The Challenge of the Gospel
Reflections on the Sunday Gospels

Cycle C

JOSEPH A. SLATTERY

ST PAULS

Alba
House

Library of Congress Cataloging-in-Publication Data

Slattery, Joseph A.
  The challenge of the Gospel : reflections on the Sunday Gospels / Joseph A. Slattery.
     p. cm.
  Includes bibliographical references and index.
  ISBN 0-8189-0969-2 (set) — ISBN 0-8189-0966-8 (v. 1) — ISBN 0-8189-0967-6 (v. 2)
— ISBN 0-8189-0968-4 (v. 3)
  1. Church year sermons. 2. Catholic Church—Sermons. 3. Sermons, American—21st
century. 4. Bible. N.T. Gospels—Sermons. I. Title.

  BX1756.S56C48 2004
  251'.6—dc22
                            2004003065

Produced and designed in the United States of America by the
Fathers and Brothers of the Society of St. Paul,
2187 Victory Boulevard, Staten Island, New York 10314-6603,
as part of their communications apostolate.

ISBN: 0-8189-0966-8 The Challenge of the Gospel, Cycle A
ISBN: 0-8189-0967-6 The Challenge of the Gospel, Cycle B
ISBN: 0-8189-0968-4 The Challenge of the Gospel, Cycle C
ISBN: 0-8189-0969-2 The Challenge of the Gospel, 3 Vols.

Printing Information:

Current Printing - first digit   1   2   3   4   5   6   7   8   9   10

Year of Current Printing - first year shown

2006   2007   2008   2009   2010   2011   2012   2013   2014   2015

THE CHALLENGE OF THE GOSPEL
Cycle C

TABLE OF CONTENTS

Table of Contents

Table of Contents

Biblical Abbreviations

OLD TESTAMENT

Genesis	Gn	Nehemiah	Ne	Baruch	Ba
Exodus	Ex	Tobit	Tb	Ezekiel	Ezk
Leviticus	Lv	Judith	Jdt	Daniel	Dn
Numbers	Nb	Esther	Est	Hosea	Ho
Deuteronomy	Dt	1 Maccabees	1 M	Joel	Jl
Joshua	Jos	2 Maccabees	2 M	Amos	Am
Judges	Jg	Job	Jb	Obadiah	Ob
Ruth	Rt	Psalms	Ps	Jonah	Jon
1 Samuel	1 S	Proverbs	Pr	Micah	Mi
2 Samuel	2 S	Ecclesiastes	Ec	Nahum	Na
1 Kings	1 K	Song of Songs	Sg	Habakkuk	Hab
2 Kings	2 K	Wisdom	Ws	Zephaniah	Zp
1 Chronicles	1 Ch	Sirach	Si	Haggai	Hg
2 Chronicles	2 Ch	Isaiah	Is	Malachi	Ml
Ezra	Ezr	Jeremiah	Jr	Zechariah	Zc
		Lamentations	Lm		

NEW TESTAMENT

Matthew	Mt	Ephesians	Eph	Hebrews	Heb
Mark	Mk	Philippians	Ph	James	Jm
Luke	Lk	Colossians	Col	1 Peter	1 P
John	Jn	1 Thessalonians	1 Th	2 Peter	2 P
Acts	Ac	2 Thessalonians	2 Th	1 John	1 Jn
Romans	Rm	1 Timothy	1 Tm	2 John	2 Jn
1 Corinthians	1 Cor	2 Timothy	2 Tm	3 John	3 Jn
2 Corinthians	2 Cor	Titus	Tt	Jude	Jude
Galatians	Gal	Philemon	Phm	Revelation	Rv

FIRST SUNDAY OF ADVENT

Jr 33:14-16   1 Th 3:12-4:2   Lk 21:25-28:34-36

The season of Advent invites us to reorient the direction of our lives

We live in a fast-moving society that has little patience with delay. We're used to rush orders, fast food, instant puddings and instant communication. Most people seem to be in a hurry. Time-saving devices are highly valued and workers are often expected to keep up with fast-moving assembly lines. Traffic jams, and the resulting delays, can lead to violent outbursts of anger. In our culture, waiting does not sit well with people. It is constant activity and getting things done, and done quickly, that are prized the most.

In this context, how does one approach the season of Advent that proposes four weeks of waiting in preparation for Christmas? At this time, we are all being bombarded every day with messages telling us to hurry, because there are only so many shopping days to Christmas remaining. How does one convince people, who are under great pressure from the powerful and persuasive modern media, of the redemptive value of waiting? Might it not be better to declare victory for the culture, embrace shopping for Christmas as the generally accepted purpose of the Advent season, and try to persuade people to redeem their shopping sprees by buying a spiritual book or two or doing a little almsgiving? Has Advent waiting become merely lip service to a long-abandoned practice for most people?

Yes, Advent is one of those times when it can seem that the Church inhabits quite a different place from the world "out there." If we think about it, it brings home to us the fact that many Christians have divided loyalties — one foot in the world, so to speak, and one foot in the realm of the spirit. Are we supposed to go through life trying to balance this tension, with sometimes the values of the world winning out, and occasionally the values of the spirit? I don't think so. The Church is in the world. The truth of the Gospel is meant to shed light on the meaning of our experience, and the values of the Gospel are meant to provide a guideline for our daily living in the world. Our faith should not make us divided persons, but should be a source of inner unity that brings together what we experience and what we believe.

Maybe some of you are familiar with the well-known play, *Waiting for Godot*, by Samuel Beckett. The play portrays a world without God, in which human existence is meaningless. Two tramps return to the same place each day to wait for Godot, who never actually arrives. Throughout the play, the tramps remain stupidly cheerful, seeking to distract themselves in pointless activities. The message of the play is that human beings have nothing else to do but distract themselves from the meaninglessness of their situation. They must persist in meaningless action or perish. In essence, *Waiting for Godot* is a play about two vagabonds who impose a pattern on the emptiness of life by waiting.

Could it be true that our culture is inviting us to impose a pattern on the emptiness of our lives by shopping? Isn't it true that it has been very successful in distracting us from giving much more than lip service to the Advent spirit of waiting? Many people's lives today hover on the edge of meaninglessness. Issues having to do with material success, e.g., a better lifestyle, a better car, a better vacation, how to be "number one" — issues that can never satisfy us in the long term — occupy many people's time and energy much more than spiritual issues such as developing a closer relationship with God, concern for the poor, respect for human life at all its stages, achieving peace and human rights for all, etc.

And this is where we get to the nub of what Advent is really all about. What the season of Advent is really about is an invitation to listen to the Gospel's challenge to reorient the direction of our lives — to make a new beginning as we begin a new Church year. And that is perhaps why the opposition between Gospel and culture stands out in a very visible way as Advent begins. If the culture wins this battle, it will have succeeded in replacing the values of the spirit with an orgy of spending and celebrating. On the other hand, if the Gospel wins, the orgy of spending and celebrating will be replaced by a festival of the spirit that might touch the deepest longings of our hearts — a thing that would be very bad for business, because we would then realize that there are other priorities for the use of our resources. So it's really a life and death battle — a battle to the finish — that we're talking about here. There will never be peace between the spirit of the Gospel and the cultural prostitution of the Christian season of Advent.

I'm talking here about some basic issues that all Christians have to face: are we looking for "cheap grace" — religion at a discount — or are we willing to be challenged by the price of discipleship? Jesus tells us in the Gospel we just heard: "Be on guard so that your hearts are not weighed down with dissipation and drunkenness and the worries of this life.... Be alert at all times, praying that you may have the strength to stand before the Son of Man." It's a frightening message about our accountability for what we do with our time. It's a reminder that a day will come when we will have to review it all in the light of God's judgment. Is it possible now, today, that waiting for the Messiah can begin to take priority in our lives — that growing spiritually can begin to mean something more to us than it has heretofore — that we can let go of some things that are really not important? Prayer, Scripture reading, spending more time with family, visiting the sick and lonely, helping the poor, cultivating a simpler lifestyle, slowing down — these are some ways to express the fact that we are waiting and longing for the blessings of the Messiah. To accept that message, we may have to make a conscious break with some of the media messages we're hearing. After all, the peace and joy of the Gospel do come at a price.

SECOND SUNDAY OF ADVENT

Ba 5:1-9   Ph 1:4-6, 8-11   Lk 3:1-6

We're never alone when we respond to the challenge
to grow spiritually

Different cultures have their own ways of announcing the arrival of a very important person. In America, the band plays *Hail to the Chief*; in Britain, the royal standard is run up; in Africa, drums are beaten, people dance and women ululate. The Bible too has its own special way of announcing the arrival of an important person on the threshold of history, but, because it's not familiar to most people, we can easily miss it. The importance of such an event is signaled in the Scriptures by noting the date on which it took place, and sometimes other circumstances as well. For example, we're told that Isaiah received his call to be a prophet "in the year king Uzziah died." In the case of the prophet Jeremiah, we're told that the word of the Lord first came to him "in the days of Josiah, son of Amon, king of Judah, in the thirteenth year of his reign." Likewise, Amos received his call to prophecy "in the days of Uzziah, king of Judah, and in the days of Jeroboam, son of Joash, king of Israel, two years before the earthquake." When we listen to today's Gospel reading, in the course of which the author goes into great detail — in fact he gives us six historical references to mark the entry of John the Baptist onto the stage of history — we know we are dealing with the arrival of a very important person indeed.

This announcement is followed by a simple statement: "The word of God was spoken to John son of Zechariah in the desert." Again, we must bear in mind that there is a rich history behind this brief statement. We need to pause a moment and let its meaning sink in. First of all, it means that John, to whom the word of God is now addressed, is a prophet — one of a long line of prophets who preceded him during the course of Israel's history. The New Testament doesn't tell us what it meant to John to receive this direct communication from God, but many of its early readers would have had a good idea because of their familiarity with the Old Testament prophets. They would have known, for example, that after the word of God came to the prophet Ezekiel, he sat speechless for seven days. After Isaiah found himself in the presence of the majesty of Yahweh, he thought he was about to die. Jeremiah was afraid he would fail, because he was very young. But after God had confirmed their vocation, the prophets stood, sometimes alone, against the evils of the day, condemning the leaders of the people and even kings who were unfaithful. Isaiah warned King Hezekiah that he was about to die; Amos prophesied that King Jeroboam would die by the sword, and that the people of Israel would go into exile; Jeremiah stood outside the Temple in Jerusalem and announced that God was about to destroy it. Ezekiel, in exile in Babylon during the same period, watched in a vision as Yahweh left his Temple forever. The prophets were privy to the secrets of God. They were Yahweh's specially chosen friends — a position that brought them suffering as well as joy. The same was to be true of John the Baptist. He would announce the coming of the long-awaited Messiah, he would stand in judgment on King Herod, he would proclaim that a page of human history had been turned and that God was doing something new. In the end, he would suffer because of who he was.

Luke's Gospel sums up John's message by quoting the cry of a nameless prophet in the Book of Isaiah: "The voice of one crying out in the wilderness, 'Prepare the way of the Lord, make his paths straight.... all flesh shall see the salvation of God.'" The wilderness theme has a rich history in the Scriptures. It carries us back to the journeys of Abraham, the Israelites' wandering in the desert for forty years, Moses' forty days on Mount Sinai, the prophet Elijah's journey through the wilderness and other stories. People encountered evil in the wilderness, but they also encountered God there. John would take his stand in the wilderness, like Moses in the desert, announcing to the people God's plan for them. It was to the wilderness that the people would have to come to hear God's word proclaimed by him. The wilderness was a lonely place that invited people to leave behind the distractions of daily life in order to find God. In it John fasted and prayed and waited. The wilderness was a place of waiting.

Advent could be a journey to the wilderness for us too — a reflective season during which we are challenged to face up to the evil in ourselves, to repent, and to wait for God to touch us. Our usual complaint, that it's too much trouble, finds its answer also in today's Gospel: "Every valley shall be filled, and every mountain and hill shall be made low, the crooked shall be made straight, and the rough ways made smooth." For those who hear the Lord's invitation, God promises to go ahead of them on the journey and smooth out the difficulties. We're never alone when we respond to the challenge to grow spiritually.

IMMACULATE CONCEPTION
Gn 3:9-15, 20   Eph 1:3-6, 11-12   Lk 1:26-38

She never lost faith

One of the characteristics of the modern world is a tremendous interest in people. A large part of radio and television programming is made up of interviews and profiles of both well-known and little-known people. Audiences never seem to tire of hearing about the details of people's lives, their reactions to various events and the feelings evoked by their experiences. So-called 'reality television' seems to be an effort to respond to that interest. Religious programs have also shown the influence of this development. For instance, Mel Gibson's movie, *The Passion of the Christ* presented, for many viewers, a startlingly gruesome picture in its effort to come close to the actual reality. And other movies have given us a very human picture of Jesus and Mary. Today's feast of Mary's Immaculate Conception provides us with the opportunity of responding to the cultural interests of many people today, and, instead of defining and explaining the doctrine, to talk about Mary herself.

Mary, in accordance with the custom of that time, was probably a young teenager when she was betrothed to Joseph. We think of her conception of the Messiah as a joyful event for the human race. However, it must have been traumatic for Mary. Joseph, we're told, did not believe her explanation for her pregnancy, and decided to divorce her quietly. We don't know how much time elapsed before he, because of a dream, changed his mind. How must Mary have felt during the time that Joseph was regarding her as an adulteress? The frustration and spiritual darkness of that period must have been overwhelming. No words of hers were able to convince Joseph, the man she loved, that she was telling the truth. She was completely helpless and in the dark about what would happen. She simply had to wait for God to show his hand.

Shortly after Joseph and Mary had reconciled, she left Joseph's home and traveled southwards to Judah to visit her cousin Elizabeth. No doubt this was an expression of Mary's concern for her older relative, who was also pregnant. But who can doubt also that Mary was seeking out the company of someone who had, like herself, been unexpectedly touched by the Lord's hand in a way that would radically change her life? Elizabeth was someone who could, much more than Joseph, understand what was happening to Mary. She was someone with whom Mary could share her feelings about the new life that was growing within her body. The solidarity between them is emphasized in the scriptural account of their meeting, when Elizabeth told Mary that the infant in her own womb had leapt for joy on her arrival. Surely both Elizabeth and Mary experienced that joy as they talked about what had happened to them, and nourished and supported each other as they shared the insights they had been given into God's plan.

A final picture of Mary is provided by the reference in the Acts of the Apostles to her presence in the upper room in Jerusalem with the disciples before the coming of the Spirit at Pentecost. Many years had now passed since she had given birth to Jesus. This was a more mature Mary — mature in years and in faith — the same Mary who had tracked the events of his life with all their joys and sufferings, had followed him in his Passion, had stood by his cross and had seen his dead body being taken down from it. Mary had stood her ground when most of the disciples had run away. She too had endured along with her Son the taunts and jeers of the crowd. She had seen it all from the beginning, and she knew now that the end of his human life was not really the end. In the upper room, she was a witness to all that God had done through her Son, and a source of strength and comfort to the fearful disciples as they prayed together and awaited what would happen.

As we gather here today to celebrate God's choice of Mary, we can find renewed confidence and inspiration in her life. We know that God's choice did not mean that she got instant answers to her life's questions, or instant solutions to her problems. She had to struggle and wait, as we often have to struggle and wait. She never lost faith.

THIRD SUNDAY OF ADVENT

Zp 3:14-18a   Ph 4:4-7   Lk 3:10-18

We're all called to experience God

A familiar aspect of our culture is the search for heroes, from John Wayne to the firefighters in New York on 9/11. It lifts our spirits to see people rise above the level of ordinary human behavior, and gives us assurance that, as long as such people are around, there is hope for the rest of us.

This need for a hero has probably always been present in people. We see an example of it in today's Gospel, as people crowd around John the Baptist to ask his advice about what they should do in order to please God. John willingly gives advice to all who ask — tax collectors, soldiers and people in general. There is nothing unusual or original about the advice he gives them. What is worthy of noting is the fact that John doesn't stop with the advice requested — he directs them to get ready for someone much greater than he who is about to arrive on the scene. This person will be filled with the fire of the Holy Spirit, and his arrival will bring judgment on the people. In other words, John is preparing them for the spiritual challenges ahead. He wants them not only to observe the Law, but also to be ready for a further and more challenging step on their spiritual journey.

That's a basic part of the Church's Advent message — an invitation to take another step in our spiritual journey, our journey to God. What might that mean? Many Catholics have been conditioned to believe that religious experience — the experience of God — is mostly something for people in monasteries and convents. We have a healthy suspicion of televangelists who claim to have a message from God, who tell their audiences "God told me to do such and such" — and rightly so. But the result of this attitude has been that many or most of us tend to limit our thinking about spiritual growth to such things, for example, as forgiving someone who has offended us, helping the poor, or going to a Scripture sharing group or a weekday Mass. All these practices are excellent, but there's something more important, because we're all invited to move from a life that's more centered on self to a life that's centered on God. We're called to experience God. We can't make it happen, of course, but if we make a start on this journey we can be sure that God will meet us on the way. Let me list a few things that might be helpful.

The first thing is to reflect upon the life of Jesus and get to know him as a real person. Start opening up the New Testament regularly and, in your imagination, seat yourself in a quiet corner close to where Jesus is, and watch him as he, for example, observes the widow putting her tiny coin in the Temple offering box, or feeds the multitude in the desert, or organizes a cookout for his disciples by the shore of Lake Galilee after they return from fishing all night. Little by little you'll get more comfortable in his presence. A dialogue may even get started between the two of you.

Secondly, ask yourself: What motivated Jesus to do and say what he did? Tell him that you want to be motivated also to bring in the Kingdom of God — to build a community of love and truth and justice on our earth. As you receive new life from him, try to be a person who brings life to other people, rather than a person who drains life from them.

Next, examine yourself about your own motivations. What motivates you when you perform acts of service, or go to church meetings? Jesus did not protect himself from pain as he went about preaching the Kingdom of God. Are you willing to be vulnerable like him, to say things sometimes that people don't want to hear? Tell the Lord that you want to have the same motivation as he did during his time on earth.

Stop worrying about what people think about you. Move beyond your need for attention, praise, recognition, affirmation, and status. Motivate yourself by concentrating on something better — trying to live in the spirit of God's Kingdom. Accept being ignored sometimes. Have patience with yourself, discipline yourself and be willing to work at this task, and wait for it to produce fruit. Wait for God.

Third Sunday of Advent

Those of us who are older can remember a time when our faith was supported by an elaborate religious structure — devotional practices such as forty hours, benediction, Marian devotions, abstinence on Fridays and special prayer days such as All Souls. Now that these things are less in evidence than before, we are faced with the question: Was our faith merely in the comfortable and familiar structures, or did we actually reach out to the holy and mysterious God behind them?

Two thousand years ago, John the Baptist gave some predictable advice to those who asked for it, but he also pointed them forward towards a holy and mysterious God who was about to enter their lives in a new way. That's what Advent should be doing for us too.

FOURTH SUNDAY OF ADVENT

Mi 5:1-4a   Heb 10:5-10   Lk 1:39-45

Have we been on 'auto pilot' where our faith is concerned?

Studies have shown that for a considerable part of each day, we are, so to speak, on 'auto pilot'. In other words, we are not focused on what is going on around us at the present moment. This happens because, after we become accustomed to a certain routine, we learn that we can actually perform tasks with no concentration at all — we can go through the motions, very often without anybody else's being aware of it. This is good for our bodies and our general health, because when we are on 'auto pilot' we conserve energy, relax more and experience no stress. For example, we may attend a meeting, go to church, drive a considerable distance, or even give a speech, and find later that we are not able to account for what went on while we were actually performing those activities. Because we were on 'auto pilot' at the time, we later discover that our mind is a total blank with regard to them.

The 'auto pilot' certainly benefits us at times, but it can be a major barrier to effectiveness in our work. We can't learn from experience when we're not focused on what we are experiencing. Even more than that, it's a major barrier to spiritual growth. This is because spiritual growth demands that we be aware of what we are experiencing. There's no such thing as automatic spiritual growth. The saints seem to have been very focused people — focused in terms of what was really happening in their lives, and focused in terms of knowing themselves as they actually were before God.

These considerations bring me to the words Elizabeth spoke to Mary in today's Gospel reading: "Blessed is she who trusted that the Lord's words to her would be fulfilled." Both Mary and Elizabeth seemed to have been very much aware of what God was doing in their lives. We might say, in other words, they were contemplative people — they weren't so distracted by the everyday events of life that they had lost a sense of the sacred. They were able to focus on the reality of God's presence in their lives. They were conscious of the fact that God was calling them in a certain direction, and they were willing to respond to that invitation. They were ready to cooperate with God's plan, and, because of that, the story of our salvation began to unfold through them.

This issue of being aware of what God is doing in our lives is not just something for the saints. It's an issue for every Christian who wants to grow spiritually — it's an issue for us. Of course, if we take it seriously, it will cause conflict for us — it will put us in tension with some aspects of our own culture, because a materialistic culture denies the existence of spiritual reality. What is real for such a culture is what can be seen and touched and felt. God is rarely recognized in the media or the market. The values communicated to us through the mass media come from a world in which God is rarely acknowledged as a player. Likewise, the strictly profit-oriented values of the market place leave little room for God. The political and military spheres of life occasionally acknowledge God on formal occasions, but there is often little or no relationship between the values of faith, such as love for the poor, compassion, justice for the alien, peaceful resolution of conflicts, and the political and military decisions that are being made every day.

The world we live in, then, seems to move us in the direction of a privatized religion whose values make sense within church walls, but very little outside of them. Here is a big problem, because being aware of what God is doing in our lives means much more than getting emotional about God when we are praying in church — it means bringing God's word with us into the market place of day-to-day life, whether that be political, military, business or social.

Trying to come to grips with God's call can be a challenging, or even a dangerous enterprise. Jesus wasn't born in the Temple in Jerusalem — he was born in a poor hovel in Bethlehem, a town crowded with people for the Roman census. Our cooperation with the Lord, our discipleship, must also be lived out in the world, among the crowds. This is a demanding agenda. Is it any wonder that, for many people, church is a great place to go on 'auto pilot'? Enjoy the green Advent wreath, the burning Advent candles, the joyful Advent hymns — they can become a pleasant blur around us as we lose focus. Yes, church has become a safe haven from the stresses of life for many, rather than a place from which we are sent out on a mission.

Where can we start in attempting to deal with this challenge? I believe it will be in acknowledging that, where discipleship is concerned, many of us been on 'auto pilot' for a long time. We may want to examine the reasons why that is so. We may want to look honestly at the benefits that have accrued to us from practicing 'auto pilot' religion — from taking a merely superficial approach that makes us feel good, look respectable, and be acknowledged sometimes for our respectability. Then give a close ear to the Word of God this Christmas, and take a long look into that poor hovel where Jesus was born. And change something.

CHRISTMAS: MIDNIGHT MASS
Is 9:2-7   Tt 2:11-14   Lk 2:1-14

Christmas is a celebration of our unity with God,
with one another and with the earth

Joy is the message of Christmas — joy and thanksgiving at the angels' words to the shepherds. The whole Christian world shares that joy tonight. We too experience unity with all the joyful disciples of Jesus Christ, with a joy that extends throughout the whole earth. But it's a joy that not merely extends over the earth — it's a joy that has consequences for the earth itself, and for our relationship with it.

We're all familiar with the ancient story of creation — the story of the fall of humanity from God's grace, a fall that alienated us, not only from our Creator, but also from the earth itself. "Cursed be the ground because of you!" thundered the God of Genesis. "In toil shall you eat its yield all the days of your life." This alienation from God, from the earth, and also from ourselves has been the fate, and the source of constant struggle, for the human race from the beginning. Throughout history, people, Christians included, have taught that this alienation could be overcome, and reconciliation and union with God achieved, by despising and rejecting what is earthly and what is bodily.

But that is not true. The message of Christmas teaches us the opposite. It tells us that we do not have to turn away from the earth to find God, because, in the birth of Jesus, God has actually made his home on earth with us. The Word has become flesh and has made his dwelling among us. Jesus is the new Adam who turns the judgment of Genesis upside down, destroys alienation, and invites us to be reconciled with the Father, with the earth and with ourselves. We recognize the earth as our home, the source of our life and our energy — the place where we encounter God's healing grace. In Jesus, what is human and earthly is renewed from within.

The Incarnation, God's Son in human flesh, reminds us in a striking way that the earth reveals the glory and power of God expressed, for example, in the healing energy of new life after the destruction of a forest fire, or in the restoration of a river marred by pollution. God in human flesh is calling us to focus on what is earthly — to discover there, not only the presence of God, but also an invitation to recognize our relationship with all living and non-living things. We hear the call to see the earth no more as just a thing to be conquered, and ourselves as separate from it. We become aware that even the genes of sea creatures have contributed to our life and that we have kinship and fellowship with every created thing.

To celebrate the Incarnation of our Savior is to realize that all things are recapitulated in him — all creation finds unity in him. It is also to become more aware of the fragmentation of the world in which we live — a world of endless division — and of the fragmentation and brokenness we experience within ourselves, that leads to so much violence, disorder and destruction. Yet it is true that everyone springs from the same earth, depends on the earth for life, and eventually returns to earth. Pictures of earth taken from space bring home to us the artificiality of national boundaries. Earth is the common source of life for all.

As human beings, we share a fundamental unity that flows from our creation out of the earth, and our re-creation through the birth and resurrection of Jesus Christ. This unity must be an energy filling the Church — an energy that calls all to full participation without discrimination of any kind. To celebrate the birth of Jesus is to allow that energy to flow through us — to rejoice in our unity with God, with one another and with the earth.[1]

---

[1] The central ideas for this homily are based on themes found in Cletus Wessels, O.P., *The Holy Web* (New York: Orbis Books, 2003).

Aging is a process of healing and transformation

Today's first reading reminds us of something that is an ever-present reality for many families today — the care of aging parents and grandparents. We live in a culture that glorifies youth and good looks while at the same time it undermines self esteem with the false message that our value as persons depends upon what we do rather than who we are. This is a greatly wounding message for those who are elderly or retired. It seems to consign them to society's rubbish bin; it's a negative outlook that tends to leave them with no useful task beyond preparing for death.

No matter what age we are, we need to have a healthy attitude towards growing older. We cannot mature spiritually unless we are aware of the giftedness of human life at all its stages. We need to see the aging process as actually a process of healing and transformation. In fact, it's nothing less than an invitation to an ongoing process of growth, in which the Lord binds up and heals the wounds of our life and prepares us to celebrate eternally with him. Our culture tells us that aging is something sad and even frightening, and most of us are accustomed to viewing it in a negative way. But it doesn't have to be so. We need to develop a more positive approach because the deprivations of age do also have a gifted side.

For example, we may become aware that we are getting forgetful. Our memory is not as sharp as it used to be. We get upset sometimes about that, but there's also a more positive side to this loss, and that is, that the memories of past hurts, failures and rejections also begin to recede from our consciousness. The ugly words that wounded us deeply at one time, and have stayed with us for many years, or the sense of failure that has been a painful memory — all begin to float gently away. They can't affect us so sharply any more, and we begin to experience a deeper serenity than we have ever had before.

There's also a loss of energy that comes with growing older.

It's hard sometimes to acknowledge that we don't have the energy to do some of the things that we used to do. Yet, there's a positive side to this too. When we experience the need to conserve our energy, we begin to ask ourselves: What's the most important thing I can do with my time today? We then feel motivated to put our time and energy into what is really important and valuable to us. When we do this, we get a great degree of satisfaction out of what we actually accomplish.

Maybe our hearing is not as sharp as it used to be, or we don't see as clearly as we once did. But side by side with that loss is an opportunity to become more aware of the voices from within that we've been too busy to attend to in the past. The sounds of everyday life no longer distract us as much as they used to. We can therefore begin to focus less on externals and more on the things that really matter. We can develop a deeper sensitivity to what God is doing in our lives and in the lives of others.

Maybe there's less denial now in our lives than there used to be. A growing sense of mortality can be a healing thing when it involves acceptance of the fact that our life is going to end — that we're going to die, that we're in the last phase of our life. How much more intense might be our joy in the first flowers of Spring, when we realize they're a gift we won't always have. From this perspective, our pleasure and delight in all created things becomes more intense and soul-filling.

Growing older therefore can be a healing process for all of us. There's something very ugly about an older person who is still full of anger, resentment and bitterness, who is still blaming and accusing and finding fault, and draining out the energy of family members with complaints. Such a person will miss out on the gifts that life in its mature years can bring, especially the richness of long experience and the wisdom that comes from acceptance.

As people continue to live longer and longer and still remain in good health, a challenging task for them will be to bring graciousness, calm and dignity to the often stressful lives of younger family members, to bring comfort in difficult situations, and to develop a spiritual perspective that can find joy even in changed circumstances. A challenge to those who are younger will be to develop an inclusive regard for people of all ages and a positive attitude towards their own future aging. Within the context of a strong faith this will become more than an ideal — it will become a way of walking through life in the Lord's presence, and experiencing his benevolence in surprising ways.

JANUARY 1: WORLD DAY OF PRAYER FOR PEACE

Is 2:2-5   Ph 4:6-9   Mt 5:1-12

War is no longer an adequate means for solving disagreements between nations

This World Day of Prayer for Peace turns our thoughts to the search for peace in our times and the obstacles to achieving it. A major obstacle is the absence of a culture of peaceful negotiation in many parts of the world, and the fact that governments are still prone to resort to violence as a means of settling differences. Our late Holy Father, Pope John Paul II pointed out on a number of occasions that war is no longer an adequate means for resolving disagreements between nations. This teaching is based, not only on the dangers posed by modern weapons of mass destruction, but also on the Church's teaching, developed especially over recent years.

A major barrier to acceptance of the Church's position, even among Catholics, is that some people draw a line between, on the one hand, religious and moral values, and on the other, the political sphere which they would see as subject only to partisan interests. Again, John Paul II has refuted this position. He wrote "Precisely because human beings are created with the capacity for moral choice, no human activity takes place outside the sphere of moral judgment. Politics is a human activity; therefore, it too is subject to a distinctive form of moral scrutiny."[1]

Catholic teaching on peace owes much to an important letter of Pope John XXIII, written over forty years ago, entitled *Pacem in Terris* (Peace on Earth). In that letter, addressed to all people of good will, the Holy Father was concerned, not simply to explain Church teaching, but to point out that the foundation for peace was already to be found in the world, especially in the growing movement to promote human dignity and human rights. He saw that, in spite of the presence of evil, the world of his day was becoming increasingly conscious of certain spiritual values, such as truth, justice, love and freedom, and especially, the equality of all people by reason of their natural dignity. He called for the establishment of new relationships in human society, to be guided by truth and justice, love and freedom. Pope John's vision was an optimistic one, based on his deep trust in God and confidence in the basic goodness of people.

Today, the achievement of human rights and respect for human dignity around the globe is still something far from being achieved, while the advent of global terrorism has sometimes been used as a pretext for curtailing rather than expanding these rights. Nevertheless, some peoples have become freer, certain structures of dialogue and cooperation between nations have been strengthened, and the threat of a global nuclear war has been contained.

Perhaps the main contribution the Church can make to the dialogue about world peace today is to convince people and leaders of nations that violence cannot solve the world's problems. It's poverty, despair, and helplessness that spawn acts of terrorism, not simply jealousy of what other nations have. Suicide bombers don't grow up in wealthy suburbs — they usually come from families who have lived for years with deprivation and hopelessness. A violent response to their terrible acts will not solve the problem. The destruction brought about by rage and hatred will not be brought to an end by retaliation in kind. Surely all of us can learn from the ancient wisdom of the Chinese proverb: "The one who pursues revenge should dig two graves."

When all is said and done, it will always be necessary to remember that we are followers of Jesus Christ, who told his disciples, "Those who use the sword are sooner or later destroyed by it" (Mt 26:52). We know that the Kingdom of God cannot be brought on by violence. We cannot serve the values of the Kingdom and endorse a different morality in our day-to-day lives.

---

[1] John Paul II, Message for World Day of Peace, January, 2003, par. 7

EPIPHANY
Is 60:1-5   Eph 3:2-3a, 5-6   Mt 2:1-12

We're all invited to follow the star, but it may lead us in a different direction from what we expect

The Three Wise Men followed a star. The expression "following a star" has entered the English language over the centuries, and has become a symbol of the natural urge to pursue a life-dream. It expresses the following of a hopeful vision that inspires a person to reach beyond the self — that engages someone in a sometimes lifelong journey in search of self-realization and self-fulfillment.

The Gospel we just heard gives us the original version of star-following. It tells us about the goal of that journey from the East — the Wise Men came to see the Lord's Messiah, newly born in Bethlehem. They were faithful to the journey. They did not give up their search, even when the star was no longer in sight. They even encountered danger in the course of it, because their innocent visit to King Herod endangered the life of the Messiah and others, and possibly their own too. But in the end their search was rewarded, and they found the King whom they had been seeking. They gave him gifts, and then joyfully returned to their own country.

Most people, in the early phase of their life, might identify with this challenge to follow a star. It might perhaps be a vision of success and happiness and love that brightens their hearts and inspires them to take on life's challenges, and to sacrifice themselves for the sake of attaining their goal. How many actually reach that journey's goal is another question. Certainly, life throws many of us curve balls. We become aware of our limitations, we do not always succeed, our original vision recedes somewhat from view, and eventually we find ourselves adjusting our goals and settling for what seems attainable, even though it may be far removed from our earlier hopes.

This joyful feast of Epiphany returns us to the original goal of "following the star" — in other words, it invites us to search for God. That's something we might reflect on today. How does the model of "searching for God" fit with the course we have chosen for our lives up to the present, or does it relate to it at all? What actually have we been pursuing thus far in life? In what enterprises have we been primarily investing our energies? Have we been able to see beyond 'Church' as an organization and place of worship to the tremendous and fascinating mystery that is the all-holy God? Surely the task of supporting a family, or any other task, cannot replace a need that is buried deeply in the human soul — the longing for God? It's a need and a longing that is present within every person. St. Augustine once wrote: "You have made us for yourself, O Lord, and our hearts are restless until they rest in you."

A renewed effort to get in touch with God might begin with asking myself: What is God's will for me? What does God want me to do? How can I best fit in with God's plans for advancing the Kingdom in the world? Can I let go of my own plans sufficiently so that God can do something with me? The problem is that we usually attend first of all to the lawful aspirations and demands of our own life, and afterwards assume that what we are doing is God's will for us. In other words, if we're doing something that seems right and good to us, we identify God's interests with our own. If that's what we have been doing up to now, the Lord will certainly accept our efforts to accomplish what we ourselves have chosen to do with our lives. But if we want to follow the star, we need to recognize honestly that our life's work has actually been chosen by ourselves. It hasn't come from turning our lives over to God's control.

The Wise Men, on the other hand, left their own country and allowed God to lead them forward into the unknown. To do that, they had to be ready to let go of attachment to their own agenda and allow themselves to be led. They had to be open to surprises, to change, and even to danger. Because they were willing to do that, God revealed himself to them. Their journey is an invitation and a challenge to all of us. Whether we are at the beginning of life's journey, or even if most of our journey is over, that star is still there, beckoning to us.

BAPTISM OF THE LORD

Is 42:1-4, 6-7   Ac 10:34-38   Lk 3:15-16, 21-22

Celebrating the Lord's baptism should inspire us to identify the work of the Spirit in our own lives

There is a certain structure that molds most people's lives — birth, school, graduation, employment, marriage, children, and so on. Likewise, Jesus' life also had a certain structure. His baptism, that we are celebrating today, marks the inauguration of his mission as Messiah to the people of Israel. While it is true that his baptism had, in a number of ways, a different significance from baptism in the Church today, the celebration of the Lord's baptism does turn our attention to our own baptism and to what that might mean for us.

All three readings in today's liturgy mention an important aspect of Jesus' baptism that is also an important part of Christian baptism, namely, the presence of the Spirit. The first reading speaks about Yahweh's Servant, upon whom he has put his Spirit. St. Peter, in the second reading, speaks of Jesus as the one whom God had anointed with the Holy Spirit. In the Gospel, we are told that the Holy Spirit descended upon Jesus immediately after his baptism. In a tradition going back to early times, the Church has taught that all Christians are "sealed" with the Spirit in baptism. The term "sealing" referred to the practice of sealing letters with melted wax, which was then imprinted with the seal of the sender. This practice identified the name and authority of the person to whom the letters belonged. Being sealed with the Spirit therefore means that each one of us, by virtue of our baptism, has been marked out by the Spirit as belonging to God in a special way. As a result, God has a claim on us, and, at the same time, we have a claim on God.

These claims come especially into play in relationship to our vocation as disciples. What they imply is that God expects us to take that call seriously, while, at the same time, we can lay claim to the power of the Spirit to help us bridge the gap between our own limitations and the demands of the Gospel. Living out the Christian life therefore means that, as we constantly come up against challenges to faithful discipleship, we should likewise constantly experience the help of the Spirit in trying to measure up to these challenges. St. Paul told the Romans "the Spirit too helps us in our weakness" and also "the Spirit intercedes for the saints as God himself wills" (Rm 8:26-27).

All this presumes, of course, that we pray — that is, in addition to public worship, that we spend some time with God. There can be no spiritual growth without prayer. It's as necessary for our spirit as food is for nourishing our bodies. Baptism is our initial call to the Christian community, and to eternal life, but we must move on from there. It's when we pray that we sense that organic, living relationship with the Lord that he described when he said "I am the vine, you are the branches."

The challenge for us on this feast of the Lord's baptism is to try to identify the work of the Spirit in ourselves and in our own lives. For example, we might ask ourselves: In what way, over the past year, have we been conscious of the movement of the Spirit? That movement can either be in our prayer or in the market place of our daily lives. Difficulties do not necessarily mean that the Spirit is absent from us, nor do positive experiences necessarily come from the Spirit. The promptings of the Spirit will always move us in the direction of letting go of our need for control, and placing our lives at the disposal of God's plans. Sometimes it is life's painful or frustrating experiences, life's rejections and failures, that move us to let God take over, rather than successes and pleasing events.

At his baptism, Jesus was recognized by his Father and gifted with the power of the Spirit. He set aside his own will, and set out to do that of his Father. It's a model, a challenge and an invitation for all of us who have been baptized. And there's the promise of the Spirit to back it up.

SECOND SUNDAY OF THE YEAR

Is 62:1-5   1 Cor 12:4-11   John 2:1-11

Is the water of our lives being changed into wine?

We all know what it is like to feel embarrassed. Sometimes we say or do the wrong thing — or someone else says or does something that embarrasses us. It's not a pleasant feeling. The event that we just heard about in today's Gospel took place because a couple of young, newly-married people were about to find themselves in a very embarrassing situation — the wine was running out at their wedding party. Mary felt sorry for them and told Jesus about the situation. He gave her a sharp response. His plans were a matter between his Father and himself, he told her, and Mary was not part of that. But Jewish mothers, they say, usually get their way, and Mary knew her son. So she gave orders to the servants to do whatever Jesus would tell them. They did exactly that, and, the result, John tells us, was that Jesus "revealed his glory."

We might pause for a moment here and ask what exactly John means when he tells us that Jesus "revealed his glory." Certainly, Jesus gave glory to God by what he did, but there's a lot more being said here. John's Gospel is a highly symbolic one, and much of that symbolism is buried in the Old Testament. "Glory" is a reference to the nineteenth chapter of the Book of Exodus, where Yahweh revealed his glory in thunder and lightning and earthquake and fire on Mount Sinai, on the occasion of his giving the Ten Commandments to Moses. That was how the God of the Covenant revealed his glory.

St. John is telling us today that we're standing on a new Sinai — that the glory of God is being revealed once again in Jesus — and the difference between those two events is as great as that between water and wine. Water is essential for survival, but wine brings joy and celebration. Water maintains life — wine enriches it. The wine of Cana symbolizes the New Covenant in Jesus Christ — the New Law that was given in the Sermon on the Mount — and the gifts of the Spirit that enrich the lives of faithful disciples, as we heard in the second reading.

So, as we reflect on this marvelous story about Mary and Jesus caring for a young, newly-married couple in a very special way — and how, at the same time, something new was revealed about God's relationship with us — we might ask ourselves: Have we actually drunk from the wine of the New Covenant — or are we surviving on the water of the Old? For example, are we satisfied with the Commandments' "You shall not kill," or have we taken seriously the words of Jesus about being angry with a brother or sister? Do we want an eye for an eye — or have we heard the words of the Lord about forgiving seventy times seven times? Do we bring life to the people with whom we live or work — or do we drain life from them? Are we always waiting for someone else to take the first step forward and do the right thing, or do we ever take that risk ourselves? Do we encourage younger people, or do we compete with them?

If we do indeed believe that we have moved beyond the water of the Old Law, then there is today's second reading to challenge us further. Are we conscious of the gifts of the Spirit that we have all received for the building up of the Church? What gift of the Spirit do we actually bring to the service of our local faith community? Or are we still coming to church with a "gas-station" mentality, expecting to "tank-up" with God's grace for another week, but actually giving little of ourselves?

At Cana, Jesus changed water into wine and revealed his glory. Today, he is challenging us to ask ourselves: Is the water of our lives being changed into wine? Is the glory of God being revealed by our compassion, our work for justice, our willingness to forgive, in the new life we bring to our community, in the joy we bring to the tasks of our daily life and to the people around us?

*We too are being invited to leave Babylon behind and journey
towards the Promised Land*

There's a big difference between a house and a home. A house is just a house, but a home, as they say, is where they *have* to take us in whenever we show up. Home is where we can be ourselves, without any pretense. We're all familiar with the experience of coming home. Much of the time, we probably take it for granted, but there have been special homecomings in most of our lives. When we've been away from home from some time, maybe far away, and we come back once again to the familiar faces and places — it's a special feeling that we don't encounter anywhere else.

The first reading that we just heard is about a homecoming. In the sixth century before Christ, Jerusalem was destroyed, and many of the people were taken away into exile in Babylon. It was a bad time for the Jews. They didn't know if they would ever see their country again, and most of them didn't. During those fifty years of exile, they settled down in Babylon. They even forgot their own Hebrew language, but they never forgot Jerusalem. One of the psalms written in Babylon says: "If I forget you, Jerusalem, let my right hand wither; let my tongue stick to the roof of my mouth if I place not Jerusalem above all my joy" (Ps 137:5-6). But the time came when Cyrus, king of the Persians, captured Babylon and issued a decree allowing the Jews to return home. Many of them did, to find Jerusalem still in ruins, overgrown with weeds.

And so, we come to the scene described in today's first reading. It's a description of a homecoming celebration. The people had many things to do amid the ruins of Jerusalem, but they could not feel at home until they had first come together to hear the word of God proclaimed in their own homeland. They listened for hours, and wept with emotion. Ezra and Nehemiah told them not to cry, not to be sad, but to go home and celebrate with great joy. It was a homecoming, not just to the Promised Land; it was a homecoming to their

God. In returning to Jerusalem, they rediscovered in a very dramatic way what it meant to be called God's people.

Today, God is calling all of us from Babylon back to the Promised Land. And most of us have been in Babylon — we know what sin is. In Babylon, money is god, or sex, or power or alcohol or drugs. Babylon is a place of slavery. And the Lord is calling each one of us today to leave Babylon behind and set out for the Promised Land. The journey may be long — it may be difficult — because it's a journey to discover our true selves. It will mean taking an honest and painful look at ourselves. We will have to confront the false cultural messages that have led us astray — the messages that keep on telling us that human worth and human value are to be found in such things as money, power, physical beauty or physical strength, popularity or winning. These messages are false. It's in the Gospel we find true value, and it has to do with God's Son dying on a cross for us. That's where we may see what each one of us is truly worth.

It's in the Gospel also that we find our true dignity as human beings. When the returned exiles gathered together at the Water Gate in Jerusalem to hear God's word, they remembered how God had called them in the past, they celebrated what God was actually doing in their present, and, in doing that, they found strength and courage to face the tasks of the future. That's what we are doing right now. In listening to the Good News we discover in deeper ways who we really are, and we continue to respond to the Lord's invitation to leave Babylon behind and make our own journey towards the Promised Land.

FOURTH SUNDAY OF THE YEAR
Jr 1:4-5, 17-19   1 Cor 12:31-13:13   Lk 4:21-30

Do we listen to the preacher, shake his hand, and then continue with business as usual?

What impact does preaching have on people? Has a homily you have heard ever changed your life, or had any influence at all? Consider the television preachers in their thousand dollar suits — has preaching perhaps become a kind of entertainment today? It's a respectable thing to go to church on Sunday, and many respectable people do it. It may look good on one's resume that one belongs to a church, but at the end of the day, what does it all mean? What is it all worth?

In the first and third readings we just heard, we have two examples of preachers — Jeremiah and Jesus — whose preaching was rejected by many of the people who listened to them. The prophet Jeremiah preached in Jerusalem at a time when a large foreign army from Babylon was organizing itself to travel westwards on a journey of conquest, and Jerusalem was directly in its path. Jeremiah's message to the people in Jerusalem was: "Lay down your weapons and make peace — trust instead in God." But the leaders of Israel responded by charging that Jeremiah was undermining the morale of the soldiers. They had him thrown into a well and left there to die, but he was rescued by a friend. Jesus was clearly frustrated by the people's attitude to him in today's Gospel. What he was saying to them was, "You think you're so special — so beloved of God — but it was actually to foreigners that Yahweh showed his special concern in the past." So the people got angry, and tried to kill Jesus.

But there's one positive thing that can be said about the people who attacked Jeremiah and Jesus — at least they listened and understood and responded to what they had heard. They didn't like what they heard, and so they responded in a violent way. But, at the least, they paid attention to what the preacher was saying, and they responded to it. They had noticed a huge difference between what was being preached and what they actually believed, and how they lived out their beliefs. So they realized that they had to make a decision: either listen to the preacher and change their lives — or finish him off, so they wouldn't have to listen to him again.

What I appreciate about these stories is this: after people had listened to Jeremiah and Jesus, they clearly saw that they had two choices: either to listen and change their lives, or else, to eliminate the preacher — and they weren't ready to change their lives. Violence is always to be rejected, but, it seems to me, there was a certain deadly honesty about all that. Because, as we all know, there is a middle course they could have opted for — it's called hypocrisy. They could have listened to the preacher, shaken his hand afterwards, even praised his message, and then continued with business as usual — adultery, drunkenness, violence, stealing, lying, abusing, hating, cheating, gossiping, dominating others, planning to make war and so on. Yes, while it has to be acknowledged that what they did to Jeremiah and Jesus was certainly evil, it must also be acknowledged that there was some honesty in their reaction.

As we gather here today, we're a long way from the times of Jeremiah and Jesus. Preachers don't usually get killed for what they say, except for a number of priests and nuns in third world countries who demand justice for the poor. But it seems to me that the middle course of action has become very popular. Many people still listen to preachers today — it can even be entertaining. But how many people really reflect on the difference between what is being preached and how they live their lives? How many people decide to change because of what they have heard? That is indeed another question.

Jeremiah and Jesus were both in the business of getting people to change. That's still why we preach the Gospel today, and I'll make two final points about it. The basic change to Gospel values that we are challenged to make is called 'conversion of life'. That happens when we begin to change some of our attitudes and habits, and come to grips with the daily task of living a Gospel life. The second change has to do with looking at the larger picture and recognizing, for example, that more than two thirds of the earth's resources are consumed in western countries. Such consumption, even in nations that produce most of these resources, is a signal injustice to the needy people of the world. For God has given the earth to all its people that they might enjoy its fruits. Most public officials don't seem to care very much about that, and by implication, those who elect them too. People who listen to the Gospel must work to change that situation. We can get very excited about sports events, but would we ever get that excited about millions of people in Africa dying of starvation, violence and AIDS?

As we reflect on today's Gospel, we must ask ourselves: Are we really interested in changing our hearts and our lives? Or have we chosen the middle course — shake the preacher's hand and change nothing? Perhaps honesty might demand that we too ought to consider pushing the preacher over a cliff. At least it would show that we heard the message — and did something about it!

Is 6:1-2a, 3-8   1 Cor 15:1-11   Lk 5:1-11

Are we still clinging to the illusion that we can call ourselves disciples, and hold onto everything?

Television has made us familiar with the sight of hungry people. There are countries where war or famine or drought constantly ravage the land and the people. There may even be people in this church today who have experienced hunger and want, who know what it feels like to be in need.

Against this background, what stands out in today's Gospel is the image of abundance and plenty. The disciples caught such a great number of fish that their nets were almost breaking. And that's not the only place in the Gospels where we find images of abundance and plenty. You remember the story of the wedding feast at Cana in Galilee, where Jesus changed six large stone jars of water into wine — enough wine to satisfy the wedding party for several days. That was another image of abundance and plenty. And the feeding of the multitude in the desert with the loaves and fishes — there was so much food that there were twelve basketfuls left over at the end. There's nothing half-hearted about any of these stories. They present a picture of God's Son going to extremes to take care of the people he loved.

When we turn to the story in today's Gospel, there's a second image that comes to our attention — it's the conclusion of the account where we're told that the disciples left everything and followed Jesus. Again it's an image of extreme measures. The disciples didn't wait around to dispose of their boats or to make other practical arrangements that we might have considered necessary — no, we're told that they left *everything* and followed him. The image of a generous gift is complemented by the image of a generous response.

Perhaps the thought crossed your mind, as you listened to the first and third readings this morning about the call of the prophet Isaiah and his generous response, and the generous response of the disciples in the Gospel — that these might be very appropriate readings for priests or nuns. But you would be wrong to think that, because these are appropriate readings for all of us. They're telling us about the abundance of God's goodness to ourselves. They're telling us also about the abundant response that God expects from us.

But the reality is, that for many people who call themselves Christians, their commitment is little more than the writing on a baptismal certificate. It will only come alive when they, like the disciples, are willing to start leaving things behind in order to follow the Lord. It may be prejudices, or ambitions, or status, or money, or pride, but certainly, when we are ready to be challenged by the values of God's Kingdom, we will have to leave some things behind. This is because the Kingdom is not something up in the air. It means the liberation of the world we live in from all that would corrupt and destroy it. When we are ready to put things such as money, status, personal ambitions, security and the opinion of other people in second and third and fourth place, then we can begin to put the values of the Kingdom first — things such as justice and fairness towards all, peace, compassion, forgiveness and the willingness to make a sacrifice for the sake of what we believe.

Our relationship with God will come alive when we decide to be a little different — to live differently from the way we previously have been living. That's the decision that marks the beginning of a Christian life, and there can be no real Christian life without that kind of decision. Unfortunately, many people who have been baptized don't ever make it — or maybe they come to it only when they are dying. They go through life like sheep in a herd — imitating, without thinking, what those around them do.

The disciples left everything and followed him. For us, who claim to be disciples too, the question remains, what have *we* left behind? Or are we still suffering from the illusion that we can call ourselves disciples, and, at the same time, hold onto everything?

*The Sermon on the Mount is a prescription for a revolutionary
change of attitude*

Most people, after they have heard something a number of times,
simply don't hear it any more. Jesus must have been well aware of
that, because he often told stories that surprised people and held their
attention, such as the worker who came at the eleventh hour and
was paid the same amount as the rest, or the father who threw a big
party for the return of his prodigal son.

The Sermon on the Mount has been a victim of the same problem — we've heard it before, and parts of it we've heard many times.
So, perhaps we simply don't hear it any more, even when it's being
proclaimed a few yards away from us. We have trained ourselves over
the years to tune out sounds or words that don't appeal to us, or that
don't make much sense to us. So we can look quite devout and at-
tentive as the Sermon on the Mount is proclaimed before us in
Church for the hundredth time, and not actually attend to one word
of it.

Of course, some people will say — the Ten Commandments
are good enough for me. But we need to bear in mind that the Ten
Commandments were put together some thousands of years ago.
They are the law of the Old Covenant, they are simply not the Christian law. In fact, Jesus even changed and revised a number of them.
So, even though we might be able to say, "I didn't kill anyone this
past week, or commit adultery, or worship any idols," that doesn't
give us any title to be called disciples of Jesus Christ. If we really want
that name, we will, sooner or later, have to come to terms with the
Sermon on the Mount.

The Sermon itself doesn't come across as a very appealing
message to many people. "Blessed are you who are poor," for example — but we don't want to be poor — we'd like to win the lottery! "Blessed are you who are now hungry" — that's not a very attractive message either. Most people want to eat plenty, enjoy life

and to have a good time. What about "Blessed are you when people hate you" — on the contrary, we're inclined to think we'd be blessed if everybody liked us — in fact, most of us *want* to be liked by everyone. The Sermon on the Mount is a prescription for a revolutionary change of attitude. What Jesus is essentially saying is that it is impossible to cling to the status quo — to insist that things stay the way they are, either in our own personal lives or in the world round about us — and remain faithful to him.

Most of the so-called Christian world has distanced itself from the teachings of the Sermon on the Mount. How did we get from "blessed are you who are hungry" to a situation where just the food that is thrown away in the Western world would feed most of the starving people in Africa? How can we be faithful to Jesus and be liked by everyone? It's impossible! Jesus said: "Woe to you when all speak well of you." Yes, we've come a long way from the Sermon on the Mount. But denying or ignoring it is not going to help. We could, I suppose, stop reading the Sermon on the Mount in church. That would be one way of dealing with it. But as long as we keep reading it and listening to it, we're going to have to acknowledge the distance between Jesus' words and some of our own personal values, and also some of the values we see expressed in the Church at large, and in the post-Christian society that we're a part of. There's an awakening needed in the Church today — we're all called to be witnesses. The question is, to what are our lives actually witnessing?

What we need in order to try to live in accordance with the teachings of Jesus' Sermon on the Mount is the presence of the Spirit in our lives. Jesus promised the Spirit to all those who would ask. St. Paul told the Romans that the Spirit helps us in our weakness. Without the Spirit, we cannot grasp the Gospel or live by it. We will react like unbelievers who find it foolish or impractical. But if we're open to the Spirit, and pray for the Spirit to enlighten us, we will be able to embrace a wisdom that is foolish and impractical to many.

What I have been saying, then, is that the Ten Commandments

are only a starting point. They're a guideline for believing in God and living by a basic rule of morality. But the new wine that Jesus offered would never fit into that old wineskin. In other words, many attitudes must change before people can honestly claim that they have the Spirit of Jesus, and that they have truly embraced his Gospel.

*The Sermon on the Mount should generate a crisis in anyone who
claims to be a genuine follower of Jesus*

Most people would not consider themselves heroes. Yet, in certain circumstances, even ordinary people may be capable of the most heroic behavior. For example, a story about a mother sacrificing her life for her child is unusual, but not entirely extraordinary; or of a person entering a burning house to try to rescue someone trapped within, or jumping into a shark-infested sea to save a drowning person. There are circumstances that seem to bring out the best in people, and make them capable of behaving in heroic ways of which they would normally consider themselves incapable. People often die trying to save the life of another. Why do they do such things? While most people would consider themselves reasonably decent and humane, they would not be prepared to promise that they would risk giving up their lives for another. Perhaps it is the challenge to assert one's own humanity and one's solidarity with others in a moment of crisis that prompts people to heroic actions, or perhaps it is the fear of failing the test, and having to live with that failure for ever after. At any rate, we all recognize that ordinary people like ourselves may be capable of heroic actions in certain circumstances.

There's something heroic about the Sermon on the Mount, told in Luke's version in today's Gospel. It goes beyond what most people would consider to be decent, neighborly or good behavior. A person's reaction to it might be, "I cannot see myself following these teachings on a regular basis from day to day. But there may be circumstances when I might rise to the occasion and follow them." We might term such a reaction realistic. The ordinary, run-of-the-mill Christian, we imagine, is not into loving enemies, or 'turning the other cheek' or giving away more to someone who has taken something already. This is more than flesh and blood can handle, and no one can seriously expect it of us on a regular basis.

But wait a moment! Is there any foundation in the Gospel for interpreting these teachings of Jesus in this way? Absolutely not! We're nowhere told that Jesus passed on these teachings to a select, elite group of disciples — he told them to all who would listen. It's clear, therefore, that the Sermon on the Mount, if we reflect upon it seriously, should generate a crisis in anybody who would claim to be a genuine follower of Jesus. It's evident that Jesus himself intended for this to happen, or he would have expressed himself in a more qualified way. If that is so, we might, each one of us, ask ourselves: Has it actually generated a crisis in me? If it has, we will probably wrestle with the challenge of these teachings for the rest of our lives. On the other hand, if it hasn't generated any crisis, what kind of disciples are we? How would it sound to say, "I'm a disciple of Jesus Christ, provided you put a bracket around the Sermon on the Mount"? It would be like saying "I'm a Catholic, provided you bracket the sacraments." In other words, the statement would be almost meaningless.

Let's remember at this stage that the principle fault that Jesus found with his generation was that they were blind. They didn't recognize the "signs of the times" — they didn't see what God was doing among them. Their blindness often caused him great grief and anger. Our failure to recognize the Sermon on the Mount as central to Jesus' teachings, and integrate it into our lives, also comes from blindness. There can be no doubt that our blindness too is a cause of grief and anger, because the Sermon on the Mount is an integral part of Jesus' plan to bring in God's Kingdom of justice and peace into our world. This Gospel is an indictment of all of us. It is God's desire to work through us — we are called to be his instruments in the world — but our blindness is holding up God's plans.

Perhaps, instead of excluding the Sermon on the Mount from our discipleship, we might take a fresh look at it while asking the Lord to heal our blindness. We need to recognize that our blindness in this regard is a protective blindness — we have been protecting ourselves from the possibility of making any radical change — because that's what the Sermon is demanding of us. The decisive factor in dealing with our blindness will not be our desire to do it; it will be the role of the Spirit. We must start by asking the Holy Spirit to help us. There is no other way of moving towards radical change in how we live out our Christian discipleship. When we are deeply open to the power of God's Spirit, Jesus' central teachings will no longer seem heroic to us; every time we pray "Your Kingdom come" we will know that we are embracing them.

FIRST SUNDAY OF LENT

Dt 26:4-10   Rm 10:8-13   Lk 4:1-13

Jesus rejected the temptation to show himself off to the world in a stunning display of power

We hear of new inventions almost every day. Underlying every invention is a value system that pressures us to accept it. For example, the invention of automobiles presented people with the possibility of faster, individualized transport than had been previously known. Speedy private transport quickly became a cultural value, and, before long, all who could afford an automobile had to have one. The arrival of commercial airplanes had a similar effect — the value of rapid transport over thousands of miles was instantly grasped and soon air travel became indispensable for many people. In our own day, even the most sacred places have been turned into instant telephone booths by cell phones — because some people simply have to have them with them at all times. Being instantly available for communication at any time of the day or night seems to have a general appeal. One wonders how people managed to function before these gadgets were invented! Indeed, the technological wonders of our day, combined with global advertising and mass production, serve to pressure huge numbers of people into passive, unquestioning acceptance of their value — and even of their absolute necessity.

Jesus in the desert was offered instant access to power and the flashiness of wealth and fame — all he apparently needed in order to impress people and get their admiration and attention. He turned the offer down. That is the subject that the Church puts before us for our reflection on this First Sunday of Lent. It's an issue of timeless interest, because the attractions of power and the flashiness of wealth and fame are certainly no less today than they were in Jesus' time. Nor is availability a problem. For those who have the ambition, more is on offer today than was ever dreamt of in the time of Jesus. And popular culture urges us on with the slogan, "Go for it!", although it's not a saying that carries much weight of reflection behind it.

An interesting question is: Why did Jesus turn down these proposals? Remember, he was fully human as we are. There must have been some attraction for him in the possibility of instant success. The obvious answer to the question is that he had no interest in forming an alliance with the power of evil. But that's only a partial answer. Another aspect of the issue was the values underlying these temptations. Let's reflect on each one for a few moments.

"Command this stone to turn into bread." A hungry Jesus is tempted to demonstrate his power by putting it to his own use and producing food to feed himself. Jesus knew that his gift was not given him by his Father for himself, but for others, and for the service of God's Kingdom. What about the gifts *we* have received? Has God blessed us with gifts simply for our own benefit, for our own self-advancement? There is nothing in the Gospel that would suggest that. Last Sunday's Gospel told us: "Give, and it shall be given to you." God promises even more abundant gifts to those who are willing to use what they have already received, not for themselves, but for others.

"Prostrate yourself in homage before me." Just as the Israelites in the desert had prostrated themselves before the golden calf, Jesus is invited to give up his relationship with the Father for the sake of limitless power on earth. He could have told himself that he would use that power to do good, but he was not willing to compromise that intimate relationship. Many people value power, and even those in minor positions often use their power to increase attention and respect for themselves. Jesus' rejection of earthly power, and its corrupting influence, is a warning to his followers that there is a tension between power and discipleship. If they have power, they must constantly evaluate it, and its effects on themselves and others.

"If you are the Son of God, throw yourself down from here." Again, Jesus is tempted to focus upon himself, to assert his own self-sufficiency. Self-aggrandizement is a common human failing. Personality cults are common in today's world, and are not unknown even within the Church. Jesus here rejects them. They cannot build up the Kingdom. In doing so, he is telling us to give God the glory.

I began this homily with a consideration of how inventions can pressure us to accept a value system, and how we often passively allow that to happen. Jesus was tempted to indulge in a stunning display of power that certainly would have guaranteed him people's attention. But he rejected the temptation. Instead of seeing value in self-serving actions, he preferred to serve others. Instead of self-aggrandizement, he gave the glory to God. Instead of power, he embraced the powerlessness of the Cross. Surely there is a lesson there for each one of us!

SECOND SUNDAY OF LENT

Gn 15:5-12, 17-18   Ph 3:17-4:1   Lk 9:28b-36

Our Christian discipleship must be a kind of exodus too

Today's Gospel presents us with a mysterious story. In order to understand the events recounted there, we need to return in history to Mount Sinai and the Exodus account. First of all, we're told that Jesus went up on a mountain, as Moses went up on Mount Sinai during the Exodus. There he heard the voice of God coming out of the cloud, as Moses also had experienced at Mount Sinai. Then Moses and Elijah appeared together with Jesus. In Old Testament times, both of these prophets had climbed Mount Sinai in search of God. As the story progresses, Moses and Elijah were discussing with Jesus his return to the Father, in other words, his imminent death that would shortly take place in Jerusalem.

But there's another reference implied here too, and that is to Christian baptism. We're told at the baptism of Jesus that there was also a cloud, and the voice of the Father was also heard saying the same words, "This is my beloved Son. Listen to him." The meaning of this mysterious story of Jesus' transfiguration is to be found therefore first of all in the Exodus events, when God addressed Moses and the Israelites upon a mountain out of a cloud, and also in the baptism of Jesus, when he went down in the waters of the Jordan and the Holy Spirit came upon him. Jesus' baptism was a kind of exodus — it was a passage through water in which the Father and the Spirit made contact with him. According to St. Luke, his coming death in Jerusalem would be a kind of exodus too.

Why was it so important to Matthew, Mark and Luke to put the story of Jesus' transfiguration within the context of Exodus and baptism? Remember, they were writing for the early Christians. They wanted them to see themselves as a new exodus people, and their baptism as a kind of transfiguration — a call to leave behind slavery to sin and enter into the freedom of God's children. That mystery had found expression in their lives when they first responded to the invitation to believe, and passed through the waters of baptism to a new life of discipleship — a passage that had only been possible because of Jesus' death and resurrection.

It's no wonder therefore that many of the New Testament stories are full of water and mountain symbolism. We see it, for example, in the waters of the pool at Siloam that healed crippled people, or the waters of the well beside which Jesus sat down with the Samaritan woman to offer her new life, or the water at the wedding feast of Cana, symbolizing the Old Covenant, that Jesus turned into the wine that symbolized the abundant blessings of the New. We see it too in the Sermon on the Mount, in the mountain of the transfiguration, the Mount of Olives and the times Jesus climbed a mountain to pray. Water and mountain symbolism evoke the liberating waters of Exodus and the mysterious presence of God who revealed himself to human beings on a mountain.

Just as Jesus' transfiguration was a preparation for his exodus, his passage back to the Father, so also our transfiguration in baptism represents our entry into a Christian discipleship that must likewise be a kind of exodus — a leaving behind of the things that make slaves of us — whether it is greed, lust, violence, prejudice, love of power or addictions, and the many false messages of modern culture that pretend to point the way to instant happiness — and the beginning of our passage back to the Father. The transfiguration story should get us to reflect, as it probably did the early Christians, on the meaning of our baptism. It challenges us to ask ourselves if we have continued on that baptismal journey towards the Father, or if we have taken a detour in another direction. When we are willing to focus seriously on the exodus journey, we will be changed too, as Jesus was on the mountain.

THIRD SUNDAY OF LENT

Ex 3:1-8a, 13-15   1 Cor 10:1-6, 10-12   Lk 13:1-9

We're not ready to look for God. We're looking at our watch instead

We don't have to grow very old before we come to realize there's a mystery in human life. Time and time again we come in contact with mystery. Things happen that we can't explain, a surprising loss or gain affects us deeply, or a person comes into our life who makes us see things in an entirely new way. At those times we become aware, maybe only vaguely, that we're involved with a mysterious Power. We get a hint that we're part of something much bigger than ourselves.

The first reading we heard today — the story of Moses and the Burning Bush — represents an effort to describe something of that mystery in human language. We can identify five stages in Moses' experience:

1. He sees the burning bush, and recognizes that something unusual is happening. I think it's true to say that there are times in all our lives when something unusual is happening but we don't recognize it. Religious experience is not just for special people — the Spirit touches all of us sometimes. Either we don't recognize what is happening — we're blinded by our own concerns and interests — or we begin to recognize it, but choose to ignore it.

2. Then Moses decides to turn off from his journey and come closer to the burning bush. He lets go of his own personal agenda and turns his attention to this mysterious reality. Some people are so much into their own personal agenda that they hear nothing, they see nothing, they feel nothing unless they themselves are affected personally in some way. They never let go of that attitude, and so God's agenda remains a closed book to them.

3. Now, Moses gets a warning from God: "Remove the sandals from your feet, for the place where you stand is holy ground." When we come to that place in our spiritual journey where we allow ourselves to feel the attraction of God, then we're on holy ground. Moses acknowledged that by taking off his sandals — in

other words, he stayed with the experience. That's where many of us fall short, because we're not ready to look for God — we're looking at our watch instead. We feel the attraction sometimes, but we're not willing to stay with the experience. Our favorite television program is coming up, and it promises to be much more interesting.

4. Moses has taken off his sandals. He is ready now, and God shows himself to him — he is in the presence of I AM. The God who is 'I AM' is all around us, at every turn of our lives. He wants to reveal himself to us. But Moses hid his face because he was afraid, and we're afraid too. We can't control God, and we'd be much more comfortable in the presence of someone we could control.

5. Finally, Moses is sent forth: Go to the Israelites, go to Pharaoh, and tell him, "Let My People Go!" And, in spite of all his self-doubts, and his poor speech, Moses sets out. That's the climax of the story, for Moses and for us, expressed in the word "go." Moses would rather have stayed where he was. Most of us would identify with that feeling.

If we're going to be open to the experience of God in our lives, we too have to be ready to "go," to move on from where we are right now. But even during Lent, we feel the urge to continue on our own, sometimes self-destructive, way. And that's why we don't see any burning bushes. But Lent is a season of hopeful preparation for the Easter/Pentecost mystery. With such experience ahead of us, we can still change.

FOURTH SUNDAY OF LENT

Jos 5:9a, 10-12   2 Cor 5:17-21   Lk 15:1-3, 11-32

All three of these characters — the father, the lost son, and the elder son — may be found at times in ourselves

The story of the prodigal son is a marvelous story about God's unconditional love for us. It's one of those universal stories that can speak to the human heart in all cultures, because we all long sometimes for a welcome back to our true spiritual home. I want to say a few words today about this story from one aspect — that of the part played by self-knowledge in this story and in our own spiritual growth.

First of all, there is the role of the father. He did two extraordinary things. In the first place, he did what his son asked of him — he gave him his share of the inheritance, and sent him on his way, although, I'm sure, he could have predicted what would happen. Secondly, he never complained when his son returned. Instead, he threw a big 'welcome home' party for him. What was it that made his father to be like that?

It was surely self-knowledge. It's self-knowledge that makes us realize the depths of immaturity and of real evil in our own selves. It's self-knowledge that makes us realize what we might have done, and what we might have become, in different circumstances. It's self-knowledge that makes us realize that we have no right to judge anyone. The father of the prodigal son knew enough about himself to realize that. He knew that, to some extent, his son's story was his own story. In embracing his repentant son, he was also embracing his own wounded self — he was forgiving himself for his own mistakes and foolishness — he was taking one of his own final steps towards wholeness and maturity. If he had not known himself, he could never have done that.

Secondly, there is the prodigal son. He was a young man. He knew more than his parents, of course. He knew there had to be a better life beyond the confines of his father's farm. He was determined not to spend his life in the fields, doing the same thing year after year. He wasn't going to die of boredom. He was so much into himself that he probably didn't realize that, in asking for his share of the inheritance, he was wishing his father were dead. Sensitivity was not his strong suit. He only knew there were good times wait ing for him, and he wasn't going to let any other considerations get in the way.

So, he got his way, and he discovered what many self-indulgent people eventually discover — the emptiness of his self-indulgent ways, and the utter bankruptcy of his situation. Jesus describes it in a very powerful way when he puts before us the picture of a Jew feeding pigs — forbidden animals that were associated with demons. This experience started the son on a painful journey to self-knowledge, but the memory of his father's love gave him the courage to make it. And so he returns home. He has looked in the mirror of life and come to recognize the reality about himself. That is self-knowledge. He confesses to his father, "I have sinned against God and against you, I am not worthy to be called your son." There's a joyful, fully human encounter between them, in which the son reveals his shame and sorrow, and his father reveals his unconditional love and compassion.

Finally, there is the elder son. He had done all the right things, and done them for many years, but he had never seriously looked at himself. There was no self-knowledge in him. And so he was blind to the things that people listening to this story could clearly see. In his blindness and his self-righteousness, he had no problem criticizing his own father as well as his brother. He rejected forgiveness and generosity and reconciliation because he saw nothing there for himself. He had no idea what kind of a person he had actually become.

If we reflect upon this story, we will probably find that all three of these characters — the father, the prodigal son and the elder son — all three of them may be discovered, at times, in ourselves. Sometimes we get a glimpse of ourselves as we really are — the evil of which we are sometimes capable, and the little good we have actually done with our lives, and it teaches us tolerance and compassion for the weaknesses and failings of those around us. Sometimes our self-indulgence, and the selfish demands we make of others, speak to us, and we realize that we're not actually what we appear to be. And sometimes we're the elder brother — better than everyone else, but unappreciated — blind to our own true reality, but very clear about the mistakes of others.

All three of these characters are embraced by God's unconditional love — and so are we. That's the message of the prodigal son's homecoming.

A window is being opened on a new vision of things

Popular culture worships winners and frowns on losers. Even though we might be aware of the destructive side of competitiveness — of measuring our own worth by the achievements of others — most of us still like to win. When it comes to the Gospel, Jesus is our hero, and we'd like him to win too. And so, it seems to me, it's a special thrill when Jesus' enemies throw him a curve ball and he responds by hitting it right out of the ball park. He just wipes them out and sends them packing in shame and disarray, as he does in today's Gospel. But it was undoubtedly incidents such as this that brought him to the Cross.

What's this story about? This woman, we're told, has been caught in the act of committing adultery. In other words, the bedroom police have made a hit, and they want Jesus to give public approval to their cruel sentence, in accordance with the Law of Moses, of execution by stoning. But it's not just the woman's blood they're after. They think they have Jesus trapped too. If, on the one hand, he goes along with them, his compassionate, loving image will be destroyed, and the people will lose faith in him. But if, on the other, he goes against them, he can be charged with breaking the Law, for which the penalty is death. So it's a story about hypocrisy, self-righteousness, legalism, manipulation, violence and the death penalty. It's a story about the darker side of the human personality, and the unrelenting malice that pursued Jesus even to the grave. It's a confrontation between pseudo-righteousness and the real thing — between truth and falsehood. And, if we are honest, we will be able to acknowledge that there's something of ourselves in this story too.

I suppose the event described in this Gospel today might present an opportunity for preachers to moralize on the evils of which the human heart is capable — the malice, lies, hate and cruelty that can be masked as virtue and uprightness and obedience to law. In broad daylight, Jesus held up a mirror before the woman's accusers and revealed their souls' depraved depths for all to see. He put them to shame, and put them to flight. But I believe this confrontation is about much more than that. There's something more here than a lesson about how to behave, or about the evils of dishonesty or hypocrisy. In this story, the curtain is being pulled back, and a window is being opened on a new vision of things — on a new world. It's a vision of human dignity and human relationships that looks inward to what is in a person's heart, rather than outward to what a person has or has not done — a vision that values forgiveness and compassion more than legal or political correctness — a vision that holds the mirror up to hypocrisy and names it for what it is. This story is nothing less than a microcosm of what the Kingdom of God is all about. Even though there's no miracle being recounted, the Gospel is nevertheless revealed here in all its power, and its enemies refuted and rendered speechless.

In his response to this challenge, Jesus is inviting us also to open our eyes and look through that window — he is opening up a window on God's Kingdom for all of us to see. And even though it's two thousand years since he first did that, we realize that we're still only looking through that window. The reality to which Jesus is giving witness in the Gospel story we just heard is still far away, because the kind of community of disciples, the kind of respect for all that he envisioned, still hasn't been realized. We hope we're moving towards it. And there's reason to be sure that we are, because, in actual fact, that window on the Gospel is not just something from the past that we look back at today. It *is* beginning to be a reality right here and now, because we are ritualizing it — acting it out — and making it present in symbols as we celebrate the Eucharist here together. That's what doing this in his memory means — sharing together the Word, the bread and the cup, and the Lord's peace, that signify we are all God's children, called into one family. It has to mean, if it is to mean anything, that the liberating love of God is changing the quality of our relationships.

PALM SUNDAY OF THE LORD'S PASSION
Is 50:4-7   Ph 2:6-11   Lk 22:14-23:56

The Cross invites us to be lifted up so that we can see with the same vision that Jesus had

All of us live with pain of one kind or another — from the pain of a headache to the pain of a lost friend. We run away from pain, we get busy in order to distract ourselves from it, or perhaps we try to endure it. As we look for the power to embrace what we'd rather avoid, we find ourselves beginning to learn the spirituality of the Cross — something that is full of mystery. Sometimes what we have to endure is too much for us, and we find ourselves even tempted to give up. We may be tired of making the effort to do what seems impossible — trying to change what does not want to change. A little criticism upsets us, a little rejection makes us sad, a little praise raises our spirits, and a little success excites us. It can take very little to raise us up or cast us down. Often we are like small boats on the ocean, tossed up or down at the mercy of the waves. The energy we put into keeping some kind of balance, and preventing ourselves from being tipped over and drowning, shows that we still have some way to travel in learning the spirituality of the Cross.

And yet, the crosses of the day, the crosses of the years, continue to touch us. We keep coming up against the mystery of the Cross, looking for the courage to live our faith, to respond to the Gospel call, to make sense out of suffering and crucifixion. Pain, we know, is much larger than what we are experiencing. It touches those near and far. Many people continue to suffer under the weight of injustice and greed. We hear about it in the daily news, and we see it in nature round about. Even the land is poisoned with waste and the air we breathe is full of chemical discharges.

But our lives are part of a greater reality. We live in a new world that is constantly being born. The Cross invites us to be lifted up so we can begin to see with the same vision that Jesus had. Can we discover new life, even when we find ourselves stripped of our hopes and our security? Is it really true that power comes from embracing the wood of suffering and contradiction? The mystery, the spirituality of the Cross plunges us into a deep awareness of our own poverty — the poverty of emptiness, powerlessness, sinfulness, sickness and weakness, limitation, failure and betrayal. As we make the effort to hope against hope, to love and to serve, we are gradually led into the mystery of the Cross. It may call us to leave our homes and walk in unsafe places, or to speak a message that will be rejected, or simply to *be there* in the midst of pain and hopelessness. It's easy to see the larger vision, but the daily journey is more difficult — the effort to find the kind of love that remains awake in the darkness, that speaks out for what is right when others say nothing, or struggles towards reconciliation when none seems possible.

Let's reflect for a moment on St. John's theology of the Cross. For him, Jesus' going up on the Cross *is* his return to the Father and entrance into glory. His glory was revealed, not so much in his raising of Lazarus from the tomb, or in his healing of the man born blind, nor even in his feeding of the multitude in the desert. No, his glory was revealed in his suffering on the Cross. Resurrection and new life came only after all had been lost. On the Cross, Jesus defeated the Evil One and inaugurated his reign as universal King. Lifted up from the earth, he poured forth his Spirit, and began to draw all things to himself. His Cross is a symbol of victory. It is the New Tree of Life.

We learn the spirituality of the Cross when we begin to make the transition from our own unfaithfulness, both great and small, into a life-giving awareness of God's love for us and for the world. The Cross is life, and the way of the Cross is our spiritual journey. We must travel that way in order to pass from self-preoccupation to compassion, from helplessness to strength, from apathy to the unjust treatment of others to solidarity with the suffering people of our world. We believe that, even though at times we suffer pain, betrayal and rejection, we can, with Jesus' love, keep coming back to life, keep getting up when we fall, keep reaching out for healing and wholeness. We will find a power in those efforts that will support us and even bring us joy. By our acceptance of the suffering that comes our way, and not running away from it, we will enter into our own inner depths and find compassion. We will learn to put aside judgment and harshness, to keep breaking bread and washing feet, to keep facing our fears and struggling with failure. The Cross is not just "out there," it's "in here," in our disappointments with ourselves, in our weakness and sinfulness. The Cross goes before us on our Lenten journey.[1]

---

[1] This homily was originally based upon a reflection given by Sr. Jose Hobday, given about twenty years ago.

EASTER SUNDAY
Ac 10:34a, 37-43   Col 3:1-4   Jn 20:1-9

To celebrate Easter is to acknowledge the pattern of Christian life for ourselves, namely, suffering, dying and rising

Today, with great joy, we join with Christians throughout the world to celebrate the Lord's resurrection. Happiness fills our hearts as we sing the Easter alleluia and proclaim the Lord's victory over sin and death. At the same time, we recognize too that resurrection is part of the inner dynamic of the universe, that, over and over again, new life keeps on rising out of death. Resurrection is therefore a symbol of God's transforming presence in the universe and in the world. And we broaden our celebration to include, not only the Lord's rising from the dead, but also the completion of what he came on earth to accomplish — to preach the Good News to the people and to suffer, die and rise again. There would have been no Easter unless there had been a Good Friday. That's important to remember, because we are also marking today, not just what happened to Jesus, but also what is a paradigm or model for our Christian life. In other words, when we embraced the wood of the Cross on Good Friday, followed by the silence and absence of God in the Holy Saturday experience leading up to Easter, we were acknowledging the pattern of the Christian life for ourselves, namely, suffering, dying and rising. The experience of darkness that is the absence of God in suffering is also part of our journey to new life. That journey is what is ritually enacted in the Easter sacrament of baptism — as those to be baptized die symbolically beneath the waters and rise again to new life.

Celebrating the Lord's rising is not quite the same as celebrating an important event in the life of another person. That is because, in celebrating the Lord's resurrection, we are also meant to be celebrating something important in our own lives. Is suffering, dying and rising actually a faith-pattern than can be discovered in our own lives? In other words, what is our attitude towards the suffering, both physical and emotional, that comes our way as we go through life? Is our suffering the occasion for anger, frustration, denial, impatience or self-pity? Or have we taken some small step towards integrating our sufferings and our experiences of God's absence with what the Church reenacts during Holy Week and Easter? What we are facing here is the challenge of either celebrating Easter as we would a friend's birthday or of celebrating it in a much deeper way. The birthday of a friend, no matter how strongly we feel about it, is still not our own, but someone else's birthday. Easter, however, is not just the Lord's rising — it is the offer, and the acceptance, of new life by all those who suffer, die and rise with him. We celebrate Easter not just for the Lord's sake, but for our own sakes too.

The feast of Easter, therefore, provides a fundamental key for understanding the meaning of the Christian life, with its inevitable experience of suffering. Willingness to suffer does not mean looking for suffering. It means that we, with the eyes of faith, have come to recognize that there's a profound mystery in suffering. Through the darkness of physical or emotional pain the Lord invites us to let go of our dependence on things that pass away, and allow ourselves to be drawn closer to himself. He is inviting us to let go of our own plans, of our own need to control our lives, and to let him lead us. When suffering comes our way, we can respond either with blindness or recognition. Blindness means that we see the suffering entirely in a negative way. It can make us angry or sad or full of self-pity or more demanding of others. Recognition means that we realize that the Lord is present to us in our suffering, and that he is offering us new life through it. That is what is meant by the redemptive quality of suffering. With recognition comes new life — the birth of a new closeness to the Lord, and a new compassion.

As we celebrate this joyful Easter day, the Lord's invitation to us is, not only to celebrate with him, but to have the courage to enter into the mystery of suffering, as he did, and, through it, experience new life, as he also did. It's a long way from the world of Easter eggs and Easter bunnies. It's a call to ground our lives firmly in the Gospel, and in the mysteries of our Christian faith.

*The challenge for many of us is to believe that we
actually are a new creation*

The Gospel we just heard goes back to a very early tradition in the Church. It was selected with those who had been newly baptized during the Easter Vigil specially in view. The recounting of Thomas's unbelief, and his coming to faith, was meant to renew their call to faith in the risen Lord, and that of the believing community, and confirm it with a promise of blessing.

Besides this important story, there are a number of other details in the account that merit our reflection. One of them is the description of Jesus' conferring of the Spirit on the disciples. After he had entered the room where the disciples were gathered and greeted them, we're told that "he breathed on them and said: 'Receive the Holy Spirit.'" This 'breathing' is a reference to the creation story in the Book of Genesis, where God "formed man out of the clay of the ground" and breathed into his nostrils the breath of life. What John is trying to tell us is that there is a new creation taking place, expressed now in the breathing forth of the Holy Spirit into the disciples. 'New creation' is an exciting biblical image that the prophets used to express the idea that, because people had become hopelessly corrupt, Yahweh was about to do something new to turn that situation around. For example, the prophet Ezekiel announced that Yahweh would give them a "new heart" and "place a new spirit" within them (Ezk 36:26).

On one occasion, Jesus had had a discussion with the Jewish elder Nicodemus about this new creation. He told him that a person had to be "born again" of water and the Spirit. Nicodemus did not understand, and asked Jesus if he meant that a person could re-enter his mother's womb and be born again. But Jesus was using the language of the creation story in Genesis, where we're told that "the Spirit of God" or "a wind of God" was sweeping over the waters at creation. Water and the Spirit, present in creation and again present in baptism, would be the means of bringing about this new creation.

The challenge for many of us is to believe that we actually *are* a new creation. What does it mean? Does it mean that we are a cut above other people? No, it has nothing to do with superiority. Rather, it has to do with responsibility. Jesus has breathed into us the same Spirit that he breathed into the disciples. If we want to know what that means, we need to look at the effect of that breathing forth of the Spirit upon them. There was a striking transformation. For example, in the first reading we just heard from the Acts of the Apostles, we're told that people were laying out the sick on mats in the streets in the hope that even Peter's shadow might fall on one or another of them, and bring healing. Is this the same Peter who had, not long before, cursed and sworn that he did not know Jesus? What is the difference? Peter has been transformed in the power of the Spirit! Peter has become a powerful person, full of faith in the risen Lord and full of the Spirit. And he is not hiding that light — he is letting people experience the power of the Spirit that is in him.

Coming back to ourselves once more — if we were to evaluate the degree of commitment to discipleship in our own lives, we would probably find ourselves somewhere between the cursing, denying Peter on one hand, and the Peter of this story on the other. Most of us have not denied the Lord, but it is also true to say that most of us do not have people waiting for our shadow to fall on them. We have experienced very little of the Spirit's power. Is this an acceptable situation? Has the Lord breathed forth his Spirit on us in vain? After all, we have been given the Spirit in order to bring the Kingdom of God into the world through the witness of our daily lives. That involves much more than attending Sunday Mass. What it might mean in the life of each one of us will only be clear when we begin to long for the presence and power of the Spirit to be revealed to us. Jesus has told us, "Ask, and you will receive." The fact is that the power of the Spirit has not been released in us because we are afraid of what that might mean, we are afraid of what God might ask of us.

On this octave day of Easter, the Church is inviting us to reflect on the power of the risen Lord, present in the conversion of Thomas, present in the power to forgive sins, and present in the early Christian community. We too must put aside our fears and our disbelief, and become a new creation in the power of the Spirit.

THIRD SUNDAY OF EASTER

Ac 5:27-32, 40b-41   Rv 5:11-14   Jn 21:1-19

At the darkest moments of our lives, when we've fished all night and caught nothing, the Lord is waiting for us at the shore with blessings, hospitality and healing for our wounds

It's often recommended that, if we're feeling upset or confused or lost, we can recover our balance by deliberately doing things to which we are accustomed, such as taking a walk in a familiar place, or reading a story or a poem that appeals to us, or visiting a friend or place where we can feel at home. That's exactly what seems to be happening in the Gospel reading that we just heard. We don't know how this story fits in with the other resurrection accounts. It's clear however that the message of Jesus' resurrection has not yet fully sunk into his disciples' consciousness. So, in an effort to deal with their painful and confusing experience, some of them have returned to a familiar place where they had often gathered together with Jesus — the shores of Lake Galilee. There they found it comforting to do something they had been doing since they were boys — they went fishing. It seems almost like an act of hopelessness — a declaration that a part of their lives had come to an end — a dream had proved to be just a dream, and now they had to return to reality and take up their ordinary lives again as fishermen. But that wasn't what was going to happen. The Lord had other plans for them. The next part of the story has a familiar, comforting ring to it. After they had fished all night and caught nothing, they drew in a marvelous catch of fish. Suddenly they realized that it was Jesus himself who had been standing there on the shore, watching their fruitless efforts, and giving them, as he always had, a command that would lead to success, even much greater success than they had expected.

This story brings a number of themes together — the confusion of the disciples, their efforts to find something to anchor their lives that had been torn apart by Jesus' rejection and death, their journey back home to a familiar place and the familiar activity of fishing, the surprising and comforting presence of a risen Jesus giving them guid

61

ance, the overwhelming catch of fish and the enlightenment and recognition that followed, the intimacy and celebrative mood of a cookout at daybreak on the beach with the Lord, the echo of the Eucharist in the words "Jesus... took the bread and gave it to them," the opportunity for Peter to make amends for his triple betrayal of the Lord, and then, Jesus' words about Peter's future death with its reminder of suffering to come, and finally, the renewal of Jesus' invitation to his disciples, first spoken not far from that same place at the beginning of his public ministry, to "follow me."

The whole account is actually a microcosm of the Gospel story — of the journey that Jesus and his friends had taken together over the previous few years — a story of darkness and light, of ignorance and confusion side by side with knowledge and enlightenment, of joyful recognition in place of blindness and doubt, of healing for the disciples' emotional wounds, of people who had run away and been scattered now coming home to their Lord and joining once again in the intimacy of a meal together, of betrayal replaced by reconciliation and an open confession of love, of a renewed invitation and a renewed response to Jesus' initial call to his disciples to follow him.

It also puts before us a microcosm of our own lives — of the confusion we sometimes experience, and the light and darkness that represent our best efforts to respond to the Gospel, and also the failures and betrayals that have marked our journey. It mirrors our efforts to put our lives back together and find a new anchor when things seem to have fallen apart, our search for what is close and familiar in time of loss, our need sometimes for someone to reach out to us when we've become paralyzed by hopelessness. It's a strong reminder of the Lord's presence in the lives of people who believe.

The cookout by the beach symbolizes the healing power and new life of the Gospel — a reality to which we're often blind. It expresses the fact that, at the darkest moments of our lives, when we've fished all night and caught nothing, our boat is not far from shore, and the Lord is waiting for us there with blessings, hospitality and healing for our wounds.

FOURTH SUNDAY OF EASTER

Ac 13:14, 43-52   Rv 7:9, 14b-17   Jn 10:27-30

*We must drop the sentimentality and reclaim the
true Gospel image of the Good Shepherd*

This fourth Sunday of Easter is traditionally known, from the words of Jesus in the Gospel, as "Good Shepherd Sunday." Besides the Gospel story, the image of the Good Shepherd is also familiar to us from a certain kind of modern, sentimental Christian art. We've all seen pictures of a gentle-looking young man with long hair and a robe, carrying the lost sheep on his shoulders. The challenge for us today, I believe, is to drop the sentimentality and reclaim the true Gospel image of the Good Shepherd. The image of shepherd is a very ancient one, and was applied to kings in their roles as governors and rulers of their people. Jesus is the universal shepherd, Lord and Ruler of all, who desires to bring everyone into one fold and under one shepherd.

What does this mean in terms of the world we live in today? I might mention three things:

1. First of all, imagine the Good Shepherd looking at our world. God sees everything, but there are some things that God does not see, for example, national boundaries. For God, there's no such thing as Canada, the United States or Mexico — there's just a land mass that is part of his larger creation.

2. Secondly, there's also something that God does not see about people, namely color. It's not an issue for God. There are just people, created in his image and likeness.

3. And thirdly, God doesn't recognize the division of wealth and resources in the world. He sees this wealth and these resources as belonging to *all* its people, and not just to any particular groups. All people have a right to a just share of the world's wealth.

In terms of our discipleship of Jesus Christ, the Good Shepherd, what should all this mean to us? It means, in the first place, that nationalism — putting concern for one nation of people ahead of concern for another — conflicts with the Gospel. As the well-known hymn puts it: "In Christ there is no East nor West." I believe this is especially an important time to bear this in mind. The Cold War is over, but politicians and leaders in the armaments industry are busy dividing the world once again into two camps, and identifying new enemies in order to keep themselves in business. People in many parts of the world are being pressured to worship at the feet of the false god of national security, who demands the sacrifice, not only of resources but also of a large amount of personal freedom. Christians must fight that mentality, and expose the violent ideology and lack of concern for the poor that underlies it. When, finally, the concerns of the world's hopeless and wretched people are truly being addressed, there will be more security for all of us. As far as the Gospel is concerned, we're all citizens of God's good earth, and we need to look critically at nationalism, and anything that contributes to barriers of distrust and attitudes of superiority between peoples of the earth.

I have said that when God looks at our world, he sees just people. St. Paul told the Galatians that there were no longer either Jew or Greek, slave or free, male or female. In Christ Jesus, he taught, "all are one" (Gal 3:28). This means that I am diminished as a human being as long as there is child slavery, starvation, homelessness and lack of basic education among millions of the world's people, and as long as three quarters of the world's resources are consumed in the developed world. Of course, we can shrug our shoulders and say, "What can I do about it?" One thing we can all do is to allow ourselves sometimes to feel the painfulness of that reality. There are lots of drugs available — whether chemical or cultural — that can keep pain away. But Jesus embraced pain on the Cross. Being a disciple of his means that we are willing to embrace some of the world's pain. It might be a first step to doing something about it.

The image of the Good Shepherd is a symbolic way of speaking about God's rule and governance of our world. We can't reflect on that image without being confronted by the reality, and that is, how successful human evil and ambition and selfishness have been in obstructing the coming of God's Kingdom. As Christians, we cannot bury our heads in the sand. The least we might do is to educate ourselves about the problem, develop a critical point of view and pass it on to the next generation.

FIFTH SUNDAY OF EASTER

Ac 14:21-27   Rv 21:1-5a   Jn 13:31-33a, 34-35

For many people, the actual project for which they are willing to make sacrifices is self-development

We just heard the words of Jesus announcing the great commandment: "This is how all will know you for my disciples: your love for one another." Psychologist Erich Fromm once wrote that when we think about the subject of love in our own lives, we are much more likely to think about the love we receive, rather than the love we give. Many people seem to think that they don't receive very much love or affection — that others are more loved than themselves. It's good to remind ourselves therefore of a basic fact — that the amount of love we receive is related to the amount of love we are willing to give. How much love are we in fact willing to give? What are the things that keep us from loving and what are the obstacles to loving in our lives? Let me mention a few of them:

First of all, there is self-centeredness or narcissism — that's the tendency to make ourselves the center of our own world. We belong to a generation that is obsessed with self — *my* security, *my* money, *my* property, *my* health, *my* people. As a result, many of us are only vaguely aware of the terrible problems huge numbers of people are having in today's world. For example, we may hear about ethnic cleansing taking place in Africa, or the horrific violence and rape in the Sudan, but it doesn't really touch us anything like as much as our own personal concerns.

Secondly, we pay lip service to the notion of 'salvation' as referring to happiness in a future world, but, for many people the real 'religious' project is actually self-development here and now. The sacrifices that used to be associated with living according to Gospel values are now associated with efforts to move up the ladder, to become rich, to develop a beautiful body, to have a nice house and car and lots of comfort, prestige and status. It's not that these things are so very bad in themselves. What is hard to stomach however is that they are put forward as the virtues of our day — that the struggle to promote the self has replaced the religious struggle for many, even so-called religious, people.

Thirdly, a certain degree of privacy is a necessity for a balanced human life. The question is, do we have an excessive need for privacy? Do we recognize in ourselves a craving to escape as often as possible into our own private world, behind our own private wall, to our own private projects and plans and ambitions and dreams? The reality outside of us is just as real as we are. The obsession with privacy represents a movement towards narcissism that undermines the invitation to genuine love, because genuine love will always take us outside of ourselves and beyond ourselves.

Lastly, I'm sure most of you have heard at one time or another the song made popular by Frank Sinatra, "I did it my way." Another expression of narcissism is the desire to, as they say 'do our own thing' — to do what makes us feel good, and to do it our way. This happens when we fail to adhere to a structure of values and preferences that reaches beyond personal preference and the comfort of our own personal worlds.

How do these things affect our capacity to love? When we stand before reality preoccupied with ourselves, we will see precious little of what is actually there to be seen. Even what we do see will be distorted and shaped by self-interest. Reality will be reduced to the size, shape and color of our own personal way of seeing, and we will see very little beyond that. Is it even possible to talk about genuine love within that context? Perhaps, but only in a very limited sense. People who are products of a narcissistic and self-preoccupied culture will tend to love only those who are of value to them, those who can benefit them in some way. That kind of love is a long way from the Gospel. The love that Jesus is talking about is something much more solid. It invites us to break down the wall of our individualism and create community. It comes from a vision of a loving God who loves all his children equally, and wants them all to share in his gifts. That kind of love is the mark of true disciples. We don't have to be discouraged by our failure to measure up to it. That's why the Lord has promised us the Spirit, a Spirit that can liberate us from our narcissism, a Spirit for whom we should be longing as we approach the coming feast of Pentecost.

SIXTH SUNDAY OF EASTER

Ac 15:1-2, 22-29   Rv 21:10-14, 22-23   Jn 14:23-29

We must all move forward together in a spirit of respectful dialogue

There have probably been times in all our lives when we were distressed or afraid, and also corresponding periods when we were able once more to regain our emotional balance and move forward with confidence. We can see both of these situations illustrated in the first and third readings we just heard. In the Gospel, which is from a time earlier than that of the first reading, the apostles are distressed and fearful. Jesus has been telling them that he is going to go away to a place where they cannot come now, but that he will prepare a place for them there in the future. He offers them 'peace' as his farewell gift, but they are surprised and confused that he is leaving them. They don't understand what he is talking about. They don't know where he is going, or how they are going to manage without him. They are fearful before what is going to happen.

The first reading, from the Acts of the Apostles, refers to a period not many years later. But the picture of the apostles presented there is a very different one from that found in the Gospel reading. It is clear that some great changes have taken place since that time. The fear and confusion have gone and a new maturity has taken their place. The apostles are portrayed as Church leaders in Jerusalem coming together to discuss a very divisive issue in the early Church, namely, what the Church's attitude should be towards traditional Jewish Laws. They discuss the issue and deal confidently with it. They seem to have moved quickly from their earlier fears and confusion to assuming positions of leadership in an organized community that was even rapidly becoming international and spreading to neighboring countries.

Reflecting on the contrast, and, at the same time, the continuity, between these two readings is nothing less than reflecting on the work of the Holy Spirit in the Church. In his final discourse to his friends, Jesus promised them that he would send the Spirit upon them to instruct them in everything. They received that Spirit and were changed. A group of unsophisticated people, with many human limitations and shortcomings, had persevered until the dawning of Easter faith, and, in consequence, would make a lasting impact upon the world.

This development gives us some insight into what Jesus intends for Christian people today who are also called to share in his mission. The gifts of Pentecost are still available in the Church. The challenge to us is to see to it that these gifts get used and not remain dormant. They must come alive in individuals and communities so that Jesus' work of establishing the Kingdom may continue. People can cooperate with the Lord's work in developing the gifts of the Spirit by playing an active role in their own ongoing formation in faith. They will be encouraged to do this when their right to be heard, to challenge and to ask questions is recognized. They have a right to receive explanations of things they don't understand, or things with which they don't agree. They have a right to be critical, and to speak out to Church leaders when it seems opportune to do that. We must all move forward together in a situation of respectful dialogue. Pope Paul VI wrote one time that "the Church's internal relationships should take the form of a dialogue between members of a community founded upon love." It is a climate of dialogue and openness that brings out the best in people. It is only through healthy and open discussion that people will test out and deepen their own convictions, and also learn from the insights of others. As we reflect this morning upon the powerful work of the Spirit at the beginning of the Church, we realize that that work is still continuing, and that we are called to be a part of it. It's an exciting and challenging task. We will pursue it by confidently addressing issues that concern Christians in our world today, by holding on to hope, and by opening ourselves more and more to the Pentecostal Spirit that the Church awaits with great longing at this time.

ASCENSION OF THE LORD (SEVENTH SUNDAY OF EASTER)

Ac 1:1-11   Eph 1:17-23   Lk 24:46-53

*Is my Christian service more an expression of my own needs
than a matter of principle?*

All three accounts of the Lord's Ascension in Matthew, Mark and Luke tell of his charge to the disciples to preach the Good News to all nations. The Ascension narrative therefore is not simply about the ending of Jesus' time on earth — it's also about a decisive thrust forward in the lives of his disciples as they receive the charge to continue his work. A window on the world is being opened before them. In Luke's account that we just heard, the disciples are reminded that they are to be witnesses to the Lord's suffering, death and resurrection before all the nations. An essential part of the message of this feast therefore is the directive to Jesus' disciples to be witnesses in all the world. That witness has been proclaimed for the past two thousand years. How successful it has been is something the Lord alone can judge. The official Church directory numbers over one billion Catholics in the world today. But we are aware that what is in people's hearts is a much more reliable criterion of faith and faithfulness than just a head-count — and that is known only to the Lord. However, each one of us can make a judgment in our own case about our personal witness to Jesus, and our own efforts to bring in the Kingdom of God.

Many people are involved in Church ministry today, and people seem also to be growing in awareness that the primary task of the laity is to give witness to the Gospel in the market place of day-to-day life — in other words, to transform the society of which we are a part. Is there any criterion available for evaluating what we do, whether in the area of Church ministry or as witnesses in society at large? No doubt there are a number available, especially having to do with evaluating effectiveness. Here is a different kind of criterion for our reflection today — one having to do, not with the effectiveness of our witness, but with our motivation. We need to purify our motives for ministry, as Jesus himself was called to do when he went out into the desert for forty days, and was tempted to use his position as Son of God for his own benefit.

Let's ask ourselves the question: Is my Christian witness in the world, or my ministry, coming from a principle, or is it coming from my own needs? The background to this question has to do with the fact that many people in ministry, both clergy and laity, have been found to be ministering primarily out of their own needs. The fact is, we're all wounded people. All adults, and many young people, have experienced in one way or another the painful blows and losses that life can offer. Many of these wounds remain unhealed as people go through life. Unhealed wounds create needs in us — for affirmation, for attention, for feeling important, for control, for friends, for support, for people to need us, or for ways to fight back against what has wounded us. Many people bring such needs with them into their work of Christian discipleship.

We might be tempted to say, "So what?" Suppose I am ministering to youth, for example, because I myself had a lonely or difficult childhood, and I find myself still struggling with those issues. I want to help young people who might be having similar problems. I may be able to do this, but the danger is that I will look to young people for the healing and support that I myself need. That is an unrealistic expectation, and may lead to unfair demands on young people. The fact is, we can be blind to the needs that we ourselves bring to our Christian service, and that can cause problems for ourselves and for others.

Here's another example. It has been observed that some people who work with justice issues bring a lot of anger to their ministry. I may become filled with righteous anger because of perceived injustices to the poor, but maybe there is also another reason for my anger. Perhaps the truth is that what I experience scratches my own unhealed wound, and that makes my anger much more personal. Perhaps I myself was treated unjustly in the past, and the pain of that unhealed wound is a source of energy now for me in my work for justice. This may cause problems. For example, I may be very judgmental of those who don't share my anger over a certain issue. But the biggest problem will be that my concern about injustice will tend to be limited to the area of my own woundedness. I will see clearly only those things that parallel what I have experienced in my own past. That is why some people who work with justice issues, and put great energy and enthusiasm into their work, can be very unjust in their own personal lives. They simply don't see that side of injustice. It may be because their own needs are getting in the way.

When all is said and done, it's up to each one of us to do a little self-examination on this issue. Is my Christian service more an expression of my own needs, rather than a matter of principle, a matter of disinterested service of the Lord? Certainly, none of us is perfect. We all bring our needs with us wherever we go. It's only when our own needs are the primary motivation in our Christian service that there will be problems, because we will be looking to that service to satisfy those needs. If we purify our intentions, we will give much more of ourselves, and we will have much more to give. We will also learn more of the truth about ourselves, and that truth will make us free.

PENTECOST

Ac 2:1-11   1 Cor 12:3b-7, 12-13   Jn 20:19-23

*At Pentecost, Jesus' resurrection takes place symbolically again
through the birthing of a new community into life*

Pentecost is a joyful celebration of the Spirit's presence. This feast celebrates the astonishing energy of the Spirit that, on a street in Jerusalem long ago, drew the widely disparate passers-by, from many different countries and languages, into the vortex of God's power and transformed them into a community. But the work of the Spirit did not end there, because the story of the apostolic Church is the story of a Spirit-guided Church. The Spirit made its mark on that community from the beginning. There had been a sudden noise like a strong, driving wind at Pentecost, followed by tongues of fire resting on each of the disciples. These images represent an effort to describe the overwhelming energy of the Spirit — the same Spirit that had come upon Mary at the Annunciation and upon Jesus at his baptism, and then had led him into the desert.

The Holy Spirit represents the power and presence of God within the believing community, in the individual lives of its members, and in the whole of creation. Jesus told Nicodemus that the wind of the Spirit blows where it wishes — in other words, it is unpredictable, and it cannot be limited or controlled. The Spirit brings light and knowledge, inspiration, wisdom and courage. It is also a comforting, compassionate Spirit. It is a Spirit of contemplation, a Spirit of rest, a life-giving Spirit, a Spirit of unity and harmony — a Spirit that pours out many different gifts of service on the members of the Church.

The apostolic Church, as I have already said, was a Spirit-guided community. This is clear from the Acts of the Apostles — not just from what happened on the day of Pentecost, but from what continued to happen in the early Church. The disciples soon began to share all their property in common, according to the needs of each member. When Peter was dragged before the Sanhedrin to account for himself, we're told that he was "filled with the Holy Spirit," with the result that the Jewish leaders were amazed at his self-assurance and that of John, because they were, according to the account, "un-educated men of no standing" (Ac 4:8, 13). On another occasion, the community was praying for confidence in the face of threats that had been leveled against them, and asking God that signs and healings be performed in the name of Jesus. Suddenly, the place where they gathered began to shake, and "they were filled with the Holy Spirit" (Ac 4:31). Barnabas and Saul, on beginning their first mission journey to Cyprus, were "sent forth by the Holy Spirit" (Ac 13:4).

Pentecost is actually Jesus' resurrection taking place symboli-cally once again through the birthing of a new community into life. The energy of resurrection, shown in the rising of Jesus from the dead, is now shown in the new life of a vibrant community through the power of the Spirit. But this is not only an event that happened at the beginning — it continues to happen. Every Christian com-munity, and every individual disciple, is called to transformation in the Spirit. It is the presence of the Spirit in power that makes the difference between a mediocre, run-of-the-mill parish and a com-munity that is a light for its neighbors. A community of disciples is fundamentally a unity of people who are drinking of the Spirit.

The Spirit is a liberating power. The disciples in today's Gos-pel were full of fear, hiding from their enemies behind locked doors, but their fear turned into courage and joy at the presence of Jesus and the gift of his Spirit. What is holding *us* back from allowing the Spirit to release his power within us? Very often it's some kind of fear too — fear of what the Spirit may demand of us. We have slipped into a comfortable way of life, and we don't want to change. We know instinctively that that is what the Spirit will ask of us. What we forget is that the Spirit will be our strength as we open ourselves up to transformation, and will even become a more powerful pres-ence within us. The Spirit will also bring our spirit joy, as it did the disciples in this Gospel. The joy of the Spirit is the kind of joy that cannot be taken away by the sufferings of life. It remains with us in spite of what we may be experiencing.

The presence of the Good News is to be found, not so much in the pages of the Bible, as in the witness given by the lives of believing people. As we celebrate this joyful feast of Pentecost today, and the powerful action of the Spirit in the early Church, we know it is the same Spirit that can also turn the witness of our own lives into good news.

The doctrine of the Trinity is an expression of the many faces of God

Now that the Easter Season is over, we celebrate this weekend the source and origin of all the events we have been celebrating — the Holy Trinity. The doctrine of Trinity — of Three in One — is a reminder to us that God is totally 'other,' totally different from ourselves, that the riches of God are inexhaustible, and that our faith therefore can constantly gives us fresh glimpses and insights into the many faces of God.

We are aware that the prophets and Old Testament writers had a much more limited understanding of God than we do, because they never knew Jesus, nor the Trinity. And yet, perhaps because that is so, these people seem to have struggled with God, with questions such as: Who is God? What is he like? Why does he act in such a way? — even more than the New Testament characters and writers. Undoubtedly, the coming of Jesus Christ made it easier for people to approach the mystery of God, and even to gain a greater understanding of what God is like from a human point of view. But that does not make irrelevant, or less enriching, the many faces of God revealed to us in the Old Testament. Let's reflect on a few of them.

There are few passages in the Bible that can equal the prophet Amos' attempt to put into words his experience of the power and majesty of God, and the reaction of a prophet who experiences it: "Does a lion roar in the forest," he asks, "when it has no prey? Does a young lion cry out from its den unless it has seized something? Does a snare spring up from the ground without catching anything? Indeed, the Lord God does nothing without revealing his plan to his servants, the prophets. The lion roars — who will not be afraid! The Lord God speaks — who will not prophesy?" (Am 3:4 ff). By these words, Amos is justifying his message to the people. "If a prophet speaks," he is warning them, "it is because the lion has roared, and he *has* to speak." Amos' God was a roaring, majestic lion.

The prophet Jeremiah's ministry involved him in a constant

struggle with God. He had a very unpopular message to preach —
to tell the people to lay down their arms in the face of an advancing,
hostile army, and to trust in God. He was constantly opposed, his
life threatened, and he was even accused of treason. There were times
when he complained bitterly to God, and wanted to give up his mission. On one such occasion, he asked the Lord to destroy his enemies. Yahweh's reply was not at all comforting: "If running against
men has wearied you," he said, "how will you race against horses?
And if in a land of peace you fall headlong, what will you do in the
thickets of the Jordan?" (Jr 12:5). In other words, God is telling him,
"If you're ready to give up now, what are you going to do when the
going gets tougher?"

Elijah was a flamboyant prophet who decorated his ministry
with mighty displays of power. But in the end he was driven out of
Israel, and his colleagues were all put to death. He became severely
depressed, wishing he were dead, and began to question the purpose of his life and his own identity as a prophet. He resolved the
issue for himself by making a decision to force Yahweh to do something that would restore his self-confidence. So he journeyed down
to Mount Sinai, walking in the footsteps of Moses. Standing on the
mountain he experienced wind, earthquake and fire, as Moses also
had. But instead of experiencing God's presence in these, as Moses
did, the story tells us "the Lord was not in the wind… the Lord was
not in the earthquake… the Lord was not in the fire." Finally, Elijah
heard "a tiny whispering sound." He knew it was the voice of
Yahweh, and he wrapped his face in his cloak. The flamboyant
prophet discovered that Yahweh was not a flamboyant God (1 K 19,
passim).

This feast of the Holy Trinity is a good time to celebrate the
many faces of God. These are just a few from the pages of the Old
Testament. But there is also the prophet Hosea's God, who agonized
over losing his people and cried out: "How could I give you up, O
Ephraim, or deliver you up, O Israel? […] my heart is overwhelmed,
my pity is stirred" (Ho 11:8). Or the comforting God of Isaiah, who

said, "See, upon the palms of my hands I have written your name" (Is 49:16), or the Shepherd God of Ezekiel, who announced that he himself would come and shepherd his sheep: "The lost I will seek out, the strayed I will bring back, the injured I will bind up, the sick I will heal" (Ezk 34:16).

The doctrine of the Trinity is not just words. It represents an attempt to express the multiple riches of God, a God who invites us to come closer and who is always seeking to reach more deeply into the lives of his people.

THE BODY AND BLOOD OF CHRIST
Gn 14:18-20   1 Cor 11:23-26   Lk 9:11a-17

'Consumer religion' undermines the Church's task of providing
spiritual nourishment

Today's Gospel for the feast of Corpus Christi situates the feast squarely within the context of providing food and nourishment for God's people. Before the crowd was fed, there was some discussion between Jesus and his followers. Most of us at one time or another have had a question thrown back at us, or a demand we have made turned into a challenge to respond to it ourselves, and we, in turn, have on occasion challenged the questions and demands of others. So it's no surprise when we hear Jesus responding to the disciples' advice that he dismiss the crowd so that they may find food by asking, "Why do you not give them something to eat yourselves?" What *is* surprising, however, is that Jesus must have realized that there was no way they could manage to feed that large crowd, but he still persisted in asking the question. They were unable to respond to it, but eventually, after he himself had provided food, he passed it to them and they did in fact feed the crowd themselves.

Most likely, Jesus had something more in mind than simply physical nourishment. And he reinforced the lesson he was trying to teach them by having them distribute the food to the crowd. He did indeed expect his disciples to provide nourishment for the people, but not necessarily physical nourishment. He was reminding them that they had been called to participate in his own mission, and providing spiritual nourishment for the people would be part of that mission.

Since the time of Jesus, his disciples' task of providing spiritual nourishment for people has become the task of Christian leaders and Christian communities down through the ages. It's still a Eucharistic task, because the Church's spiritual nourishment will always be related to the Eucharist, and will always, in some manner, be helping people to celebrate it at deeper and deeper levels of faith. However, there's a major factor in Western culture today that tends to undermine the Church's task of providing spiritual nourishment — that is, the tendency for religion itself to be categorized as a consumer product, a part of the so-called 'service sector' of the economy. This has meant that the language of the market has been transferred into the religious arena — market vocabulary and know-how has become a must for many so-called 'religious practitioners.' In order to be successful, those who market 'consumer religion' have to provide people with a well-packaged and attractive product. In other words, they have to give people what they want. Successful religious marketing, it is said, will engender in people positive feelings of well-being; it will convince people that disciples of Jesus can be 'winners' rather than 'losers' in the rat-race of the modern world. In short, retailers of 'consumer religion' will have to respond to cultural values — will have to make people feel good and feel successful. Market analysts give assurance that it is the religions which succeed at doing this that will prosper, while others will eventually die out.

Even though this approach certainly does not describe the Church's official understanding of evangelization, there can be little doubt that many of our people have been influenced by it. Popular parishes are sometimes identified as those with a strong 'feel-good' factor. It is more rare to read about a parish that is popular because of a powerful Gospel challenge addressed to its members. Often there is an unspoken cultural pressure on church leaders and ministers to please people and make them feel good. Parishioners who are generous to their parish sometimes seem to feel that they have a right to hear a particularly pleasing and unchallenging version of the Gospel that fits in with their wishes and makes little or no demands of them.

But religion that gives people only what they want to hear is false religion, and ministers of the Gospel who aim at doing that are false prophets. Certainly, we all have a tendency to filter out the more challenging parts of the Gospel. But the fact is that Jesus said some things that would make many of us cringe. It's much easier to preach about God's unconditional love than to preach about what seems to have been a favorite subject of Jesus, namely, the hypocrisy of many so-called "religious people." Preaching about love may be good for the collection, but it will fall short of the Gospel when the cross, and God's expectations of us, are left out.

This feast of the Body and Blood of the Lord turns our thoughts to the subject of spiritual nourishment. We need the Eucharist — it's food for our faith, and for our Christian journey. St. Paul reminds us that, each time we celebrate it, we proclaim the death of the Lord. We cannot separate the Eucharist from the daily dying and rising of a faithful Christian life.

It is the disciplined heart that will speak gracious words

Evil is not a division between groups of people or nations — it is never simply a matter of 'we or they.' It is a line that runs through every human heart. Today's first and third readings refer to the evil of the human heart that is revealed in a person's words. When we reflect on the kind of evils that are perpetrated in the world today, it might seem to us that sins having to do with speech — the evil, for example, that comes from gossip, lies or rash judgments, or remaining silent when we should speak out, is a relatively minor issue. But it may not be that simple. Hannah Arendt wrote on one occasion that most evil is done by people who never make up their minds to be good or evil. Her words were written against the background of the Holocaust and the many people of that time who preferred to remain neutral, saying nothing either for or against what was happening to the Jews. But her remark has a general application. The evil of silence can be even more devastating than the evil of speech.

Jesus' words in today's Gospel refer to 'the heart' as the source of good or evil words. In biblical language, a person's thoughts, feelings, plans and purposes come from the heart. The expression refers to those intentions and movements, either good or evil, that arise from the depths of a person, and for which a person must own responsibility. Evil that comes from 'the heart' turns our attention especially to what actually is in one's 'heart.' Modern psychology has done a lot to shed light on what takes place within people, and sometimes exonerates them from their evil intentions and actions because of destructive influences, present or past. We've seen the bumper sticker that reads "The devil made me do it!" The scapegoat was an ancient device that remains very much alive in modern times. We do or say evil things, but there are people or factors that may lessen or excuse our responsibility, at least in our own eyes. Pilate washed his hands.

Judging and blaming and condemning is a favorite occupation in some quarters. But remember that the useless life (from a Western cultural point of view) of the beggar Lazarus at the gate of the rich man was accepted by God, whereas the successful life of the rich man was not. Perhaps we need to bear in mind, when we hear of someone's fall from grace, that, whereas we may know all the details of his or her fall, we probably know nothing about that person's struggles. We don't know how many times a person may have successfully struggled against evil, before finally succumbing to it. There are few people so morally sick that they don't sometimes experience a dilemma of conscience between good and evil. Priests who have been listening to confessions for many years will testify that the human struggle against the influence of evil has by no means come to an end. The quick judgments we sometimes make about people may be based on little knowledge about the person we are judging, and ignorance of or denial of the evil within ourselves. It was St. Philip Neri, in sixteenth-century Rome, who, on hearing of someone's fall from grace, would say, "There but for the grace of God go I."

Self-discipline is one of the marks of a disciple of Jesus. That does not mean making things difficult for oneself. When we discipline ourselves, we push to one side the desire to focus on self, and we make available to God some inner space where he can touch us with his love. Some people have terrible tongues. However, it is discipline of the self, rather than simply controlling one's speech, that is needed. Self-discipline will bring balance to our decisions and judgments. Of course, it's very much a counter-cultural activity. There are no cultural slogans around that recommend self-discipline — in fact, the opposite is the case. But, when all is said and done, it is the disciplined heart that will speak gracious words.

NINTH SUNDAY IN ORDINARY TIME
1 K 8:41-43   Gal 1:1-2, 6-10   Lk 7:1-10

The story of the centurion challenges us to open our eyes to what God may be doing in our 'secular' world

As we go through life, and experience the let-downs and disappointments that sometimes come our way, we may find ourselves growing less optimistic about people, and a little more guarded in our expectations of them, than we used to be. But, on the other hand, it may happen that a person acts in a way that exceeds all our expectations, and, at least temporarily, our faith in human nature is restored. By way of introduction to today's Gospel account, we might ask the question: What would a Jew have expected of a Roman soldier? Roman soldiers were a tough body of men, recruited from around the empire, and feared for their courage and cruelty. Jews, including Jesus, would have expected little, if anything, from them.

Today's Gospel therefore describes an amazing event — we're told that even Jesus himself was amazed. This soldier, a non-Jewish foreigner, of whose faith Jesus said that he had never found anything like it in Israel, is remembered, and will be remembered until the end of time. The centurion's words have even been memorialized in our Eucharist — every time we prepare to receive Holy Communion we repeat his words, "Lord, I am not worthy." There are only a few people recorded in the New Testament whom Jesus praised — John the Baptist, Nathaniel, whom he called "a true Israelite," the widow who put a tiny coin in the Temple treasury, and this centurion. It is a very select group. The first three were Israelites, but this man was a member of a despised entity. He was an officer in the occupying Roman army that had subjugated the land of Israel.

What kind of a person was this centurion who recognized Jesus as Lord of life? To say that his attitude towards Jesus — a wandering healer from a subject nation — was uncharacteristic, is to understate the case. It was astonishing. We know that this man had been generous to the Jews, and had even built their synagogue, but that cannot parallel in any way what took place in today's Gospel — that he should have begged Jesus just to give a command, because he was certain that his servant would then be healed! The centurion did not even meet Jesus throughout this account.

If Jesus himself was astonished by the man's faith, we can only imagine the reaction of Jewish onlookers. Their attitude towards their religion was very exclusive — they were God's chosen people, and this man was not included among them. But some of them were prepared to intercede with Jesus on his behalf for a favor. They were probably hoping for further generosity from him. Exclusive attitudes towards outsiders were not confined, as we know, to the Jews. It is still strongly in evidence in our world today. Many Catholics, and other Christians too, believe that their faith entitles them to a very exclusive relationship with God. They are very reluctant to concede much to those outside the fold of Christian faith. This point of view has led to considerable prejudice.

The story of the centurion and Jesus must certainly broaden our horizons when it comes to reflecting on God's presence and action in the world. It cannot fit with an exclusivist point of view that would see, for example, unbaptized people as remote from God. It's not just a story about someone coming to faith in Jesus — it's a story about someone who already had faith as this story commences. It's like a preview of Pentecost — when many people of different cultures and languages experienced the power of the Spirit — before Pentecost actually happened.

Theologians today are actively reflecting on what God's presence in the universe and in the world means. The Second Vatican Council taught that the needs and longings of all people can be genuine signs of the presence or the purpose of God.[1] We realize that God has given us many wonderful blessings in the Catholic Church, but that does not mean that God is not powerfully active outside the Church in people of good will. Jesus released his saving Spirit upon

---

[1] *The Church in the Modern World*, # 11.

the whole world with his resurrection. Wherever genuine relation-ships are being established among the world's peoples, there is the saving presence of the Spirit, because, as Vatican II also taught, all humanity form one family.[2] We believe that all peoples are called to be transformed by the unconditional love of God, and this love is constantly moving people towards relationship. Everything in the religions of the world that moves people towards reconciliation and healing comes from God, because God's love is present and active in all his creation, and in every movement towards genuine unity. When our late Holy Father, Pope John Paul II met with world reli-gious leaders in Assisi to pray with them, he was recognizing the fact that God's Spirit was present in and working through them too.

The interaction between Jesus and the centurion provides us with a challenge to open our eyes to what God may be doing in our so-called 'secular' world. It teaches us that we would be unwise to limit real, saving faith to the world of Christian belief, and it invites us to look beyond.

---

[2] Ibid., # 24.

1 K 17:17-24   Gal 1:11-19   Lk 7:11-17

Compassion, rather than separateness, was to be the fundamental criterion of religious behavior for Jesus' disciples

Compassion is the outstanding element in the Gospel story we just heard. As Jesus approached the gates of Nain, I'm sure he had other things on his mind as he pursued his preaching task, announcing the Kingdom of God coming in power. But he wasn't so preoccupied that he didn't notice what was going on around him. He observed a widow sorrowfully following the funeral procession of her only son. It's often been said that the greatest sorrow of a mother is to bury her child, and this was her only one. A part of herself must have died too as she faced the reality of what was happening. Not only was she losing her son, she was also losing her only source of support for her old age. There were no insurance policies or old-age pensions in those days.

At that moment Jesus' personal agenda changed, all other considerations were postponed, and he approached the widow. He hated to see her tears of mourning, for he was moved with compassion. In anticipation of what he was about to do, he urged her not to cry. He touched the litter and told the dead man to get up, whereupon he did so and began to speak. Then, we're told, "Jesus gave him back to his mother." We may imagine Jesus embracing mother and son, and drawing them close to each other. It must have been an ecstatic moment for her, and a joyful one for him. The onlookers were filled with fear because of the display of power they had witnessed, and they praised God.

Compassion is a central component of the Gospel. Jesus, on one occasion, demonstrated in a very striking manner just how strongly he felt about its centrality. The Book of Leviticus had given the Jews a fundamental law governing their religious practice: "Be holy, for I, the Lord your God, am holy" (Lv 19:2). Holiness had to do with the total separateness of God from creation; when applied to the people of Israel, it was interpreted as a command to separate themselves from everything and everyone that was ritually impure. But Jesus rejected that understanding of the Law. Instead, he provided his followers with a parallel statement to that laid down in Leviticus that actually reinterpreted what holiness was all about. He commanded: "Be compassionate, as your Father in heaven is compassionate" (Lk 6:36). Compassion, rather than separateness, was, from then onwards, to be the fundamental statement of religious attitude for Jesus' disciples.[1] Jesus rejected an external criterion of holiness, expressed in terms of ritual purity and separateness, and proposed an inner criterion — a religion of the heart — that would be expressed in terms of compassion. God's compassion was to be the model for his disciples. The Kingdom of God would be expressed in life-giving relationships, in a compassionate love that would be universal, that would embrace all people — the sinners as well as the righteous. Jesus acted that message out as he went about preaching the Kingdom. For example, the true neighbor to the man who fell among robbers was the Good Samaritan, not the priest or the Levite. They had passed by lest they be made ritually impure by contact with the wounded man, and so be unable to participate in worship. They were being obedient to Leviticus' law of holiness, but they did not at all measure up to Jesus' new law of compassion. Only the Samaritan had shown compassion, and was therefore approved by Jesus.

We all need to evaluate the importance of compassion in our attitudes and decisions. A recent survey in the United States showed that, although average incomes have more than tripled in the past fifty years, the degree of personal happiness and life satisfaction has not grown at all. Jesus' recipe for happiness has nothing to do with income, but compassion plays a major part in it.

---

[1] See John Fuellenbach, SVD, *Throw Fire* (Manila: Logos Publications, Inc., Fourth Printing, 2000), pp. 200ff.

2 S 12:7-10, 13   Gal 2:16, 19-21   Lk 7:36-8:3

Are we conscious of compassion as a powerfully
motivating force in our lives?

The presentation of Jesus as a sexual being has, for the most part, been studiously avoided for almost two thousand years. That probably had to do with Christian attitudes towards sex that were greatly influenced by St. Augustine's negative views. However, modern media have made a feast of this issue in recent times, going to the opposite extreme and giving us a picture of a sexual Jesus that goes far beyond scriptural data and Church tradition. There has to be a middle course between these two positions, because the Scriptures do not, in fact, picture Jesus as an asexual human being — as a person with no sexuality or sexual feelings. Today's Gospel reading provides an interesting example. It puts before us a sensual picture that is strongly redolent of sexuality, with Jesus as the main protagonist.

Picture Jesus reclining on a backless couch beside a low table, as was the custom in those days. A beautiful woman, with a bad reputation, approaches him, actually coming physically close to him. He does nothing to discourage her. Her tears of sorrow fall upon his feet. She than takes his feet in her hands, wipes them with the long tresses of her hair, covers them with kisses and begins to massage them with a deliciously perfumed oil, whose odor fills the room. Everyone present is silently watching, including the inwardly hostile Pharisee, who already feels that his home has been violated by the entry of this woman. Surely Jesus, if he is a holy man, will realize what is happening and will push her away? What will the other guests think of him if he lets this scene continue? But no, Jesus doesn't push her away. He accepts her public sorrow for her sins and her love and affection. His body language must have already signaled to her that what she was doing was quite acceptable to him. Jesus is enjoying the foot massage and the delightful smell of the perfumed oil. There is a lengthy silence in the room — a critical silence that is full of questioning. Finally, he decides to address the issue that everyone else is afraid to address. His words imply total approval of what the woman is doing. He points out that she has more than compensated for the absence of the customary hospitality, which had not been offered on Jesus' entry into the Pharisee's house. And she has even gone further — she has offered Jesus affection and love. Now, all her sins are forgiven, because of her great love. Her trust in him has saved her, and she may leave Jesus' presence, her heart filled with a blessed peace.

In last Sunday's homily, I noted that Jesus drew a sharp line between holiness as ritual purity and separateness, and holiness as compassion. He told people to be holy by being compassionate like the Good Samaritan, and not with the holiness of the priest and Levite, who passed by. In this story there is the same clash of values. On the one hand, the Pharisee's concern has to do with ritual purity and separateness. On the other, Jesus is concerned about showing compassion and love. The woman's show of hospitality to Jesus highlights the Pharisee's failure to provide it. Compassion and love are not necessarily to be found in the hearts of the religiously correct. The self-righteous Pharisee was very critical of Jesus' behavior, but he gave no thought to his own neglect of hospitality. At the end of the story, it is the woman who is occupying the higher moral ground, rather than those who are judging her.

This Gospel, as always, holds a mirror up before ourselves. We note the repentant woman, the observers, either neutral or judgmental, and Jesus. There is one who sheds tears of sorrow, there are those critics who have no more than a legal view of morality, those who just sit on the fence, and finally, Jesus himself, who expresses compassion, understanding and forgiveness. Where do we take our stand when it comes to issues of forgiveness or justice or fairness? Are we among the observers who either remain silently neutral or openly critical, or are we conscious of compassion as a powerfully motivating force in our lives, moving us to action?

TWELFTH SUNDAY IN ORDINARY TIME
Zc 12:10-11, 13:1   Gal 3:26-29   Lk 9:18-24

*The sufferings of our daily lives can open us up to a profound
mystery — a mystery that leads to new life*

Traditional Catholics sometimes point nostalgically to the Christian
Europe of the Middle Ages as a blessed time when there was no clash
between religion and culture. In that era, religion was indeed very
much part of culture, and young people absorbed religious meaning from the culture as they grew up. There was little tension between the two. That is, of course, no longer true. In our Western
world, the gap between culture and authentic religious values is
widening all the time. There is still, of course, a veneer of cultural,
civic religion that uses religious symbols, and that serves to promote
the illusion of a still-existing Christian society, but that actually has
little to do with faith in God or Christian values. It's a kind of religion that often serves political ends. Authentic religion has, however, been pushed to one side, and is now understood by many as
occupying a very private, personal part of people's lives. It is seen as
a purely optional 'extra,' available for those who still need its 'com-
forts,' as they call them. The true understanding of religion as a tradition of wisdom, based on faith, that helps us negotiate the funda
mental mysteries and challenges of life, has fallen into abeyance in
many quarters.

Opposition between authentic religion and certain aspects of
our culture is a major obstacle to getting a hearing for the Gospel
today, because culture plays such a fundamental role in any society.
It teaches people how to be human and how to live. Culture also
forms many of our attitudes towards life. The mass culture provided
by the popular press and electronic media in our time is, for the most
part, based on the pursuit of pleasure, wealth and power. Self-development and free, uninhibited self-expression have replaced self-
discipline in the popular mind. As persons in society, we swim within
our culture like fish in the sea. We absorb many good things from
cultural wisdom, but we must also be critical of it.

This ongoing tension between culture and religion can strike us very sharply if we pay attention to certain statements of Jesus, such as those we just heard in today's Gospel. The idea of denying one-self and carrying one's cross daily is certainly in conflict with the powerful messages of Western culture. And we are all influenced by that culture in one way or another. One of the results of this influence may be that we tend to concentrate on the 'soft' sayings of Jesus rather than on the 'hard' ones. Nobody can argue with statements such as, "Come to me, all you who labor and are burdened, and I will refresh you," or, "Love one another as I have loved you," or "I no longer call you servants; I call you friends." These are comforting messages. As long as religious preaching focuses on such as these, or on promising people success and prosperity on certain conditions, there will probably be no difficulty filling pews on Sundays.

However, if we want to move beyond the level of superficial religious practice, we will, sooner or later, have to come to terms with the central symbol of our faith, the Cross. The Cross confronts us with the reality of suffering in the midst of a culture that would seek to deny and hide from some of life's basic realities, for example, the suffering involved in sickness, loss, aging and death itself. We're all familiar with that moving Good Friday ritual, when the Church invites us to come forward and embrace the Cross. What does that ritual mean? It's not just an emotional moment of sympathy with Jesus' sufferings. It's a ritual that's meant to embody the mystery that's at the heart of Christian life, and invite us to be a part of it. It's a recognition of the fact that there's no way for us to move forward towards the new life of Easter unless we're willing to embrace the Cross in our daily life. Not to embrace it is to travel on a pathway into bitterness, cynicism and even despair — it's to dry up the spiritual wellsprings within us.

We're all used to making the Sign of the Cross. In fact, we're so used to it that we often make it unthinkingly. Maybe we need to put meaning back into that ritual. To sign our bodies with the Cross is a way of embracing the Cross. It's a way of reminding ourselves that the painful losses, sufferings and rejections of our daily lives can open us up to a profound mystery — a mystery that can lead us to new life.

THIRTEENTH SUNDAY IN ORDINARY TIME
1 K 19:16b, 19-21   Gal 5:1, 13-18   Lk 9:51-62

We must live in the present, and be inner-directed, to be ready to respond to the Gospel

If we look back on our lives, most of us will recall occasions when there was an invitation or a request made of us, or an opportunity offered, for which we were not quite ready at the time, and so we did not respond positively. These memories may cause us some regret now. Perhaps if we had been more inwardly free in the past, our responses might have been different.

All the readings today have to do with the inner freedom that is necessary in order to live a life of faith. In the first and third readings, we heard a number of stories about God's expectations of some people, uncovering the fact that they were not entirely ready to respond. The second reading, from Paul's Letter to the Galatians, gives us the key to understanding that kind of readiness. He tells the people that God has given them the gift of freedom — but it's not the freedom to do whatever they want. In other words, God's gift is an inner freedom of spirit that enables us to put ourselves at the service of the Gospel and live out its values in our daily lives.

Jesus' expectation in today's Gospel is that people be inwardly free to respond to his invitation without making any conditions. But how do we know if we are inwardly free? The obvious answer has to do with how we are living. If, for example, a person is a slave to anger, vengeful feelings, envy, greed, alcohol, or sexual desire — such a person will not have the inner freedom to live a Gospel life. But there are other things we need to look at as well. I might mention two factors in particular — ability to live in the present, and what is called inner-directedness.

First of all, being inwardly free means being able to live in the present moment. Many people live very little of their conscious lives in the present — they're either thinking about the past, or looking forward to the future. Often we carry around with us some baggage from our past — regrets over mistakes we have made — guilt over things we have done or not done — anger over people who have hurt us — wishes that our lives had gone differently, or sadness at losses we've suffered. It is such kinds of things that prevent us from focusing on our life in the present. "Let the dead bury their dead," Jesus said, and, "Whoever puts his hand to the plow but keeps looking back is unfit for the Kingdom of God." Living in the future will have the same effect. We won't be able to live in the present when we're constantly awaiting some future good fortune, be it joy, happiness or fulfillment. When that is the case, the present becomes simply an unfortunate reality that we hope will pass as quickly as possible. We're simply not there! And, when we don't focus on our present, it becomes impossible for us to meet God who is always in the present, nor can we come to know what God expects of us at the present moment.

The second factor that's important for inner freedom is the question: Am I an inner-directed person? That means: Is my life guided by some conviction from within me? Or am I constantly looking to see which way the wind is blowing — what people are saying, what people are doing, what people want or reject — as a guide for my own choices? Remember what Jesus said to the people when he was admiring John the Baptist: "What did you go out into the desert to see — a reed shaking in the wind?" Jesus admired John because he was not a reed shaking in the wind. In other words, he was an inner-directed person — he was inwardly free. He was prepared to do what was right, and to continue pursuing the course he had set for himself, even though he might make enemies and face danger because of it.

That is the challenge of God's word today — firstly, to be more aware of the commitment we have made as Jesus' disciples, and of the fact that there is a cost to being a disciple; and secondly, to be more focused on the present, so that we can be fully alive and better able to respond to God's invitation, that always comes to us in the present moment.

Is 66:10-14c   Gal 6:14-18   Lk 10:1-12, 17-20

The first part of the Mass is a nourishing feast of God's word

All three readings are our source of reflection on God's word today. It was the Second Vatican Council that provided the impetus, about forty years ago, for the readings at Mass to be increased from two to three. Catholics had been starved of God's word for centuries, and it was the Church's intention, in making that change, to center the first part of the Mass on a nourishing feast of God's word. The three readings in the Sunday liturgy were meant to be like a kind of symphony, made up of different movements, played on various instruments, that blended together to make up a harmonious unity. The reality however has been somewhat different. Sometimes there seems to be little or no thematic unity in the readings. But this may be balanced by the fact that there is always unity in the spirit of faith that underlies them, that is being expressed in various ways.

Today's first reading is taken from the last chapter of the Book of Isaiah, and gives an ideal picture of a future Jerusalem, God's city. The people who have mourned over her former destruction by the Babylonians will now rejoice in her. They will be comforted, like a child at its mother's breast, not only, the prophet adds, by the great city, but by Yahweh himself. Peace and prosperity will flow into Jerusalem like the waters of a river. This reading gives us a vision of faith integrated with life experience. Jerusalem was probably not much to look at when it was written. It took many years for the returning exiles to remove the rubble of past destruction and rebuild it. Yet the writer of this passage could, with faith, look beyond that to the future and see something beautiful. These lyrical verses are a reminder to us that faith is a way of seeing that transcends the limits of human sight. What about ourselves — do we ever experience this kind of faith? Do we ever experience our faith as a light in darkness — as an energy leading us on through difficult times?

The second reading gives us a profound reflection from St. Paul about what is really important for disciples of Jesus. These are the final words of his Letter to the Galatians, written to convince them that, now that they have been baptized, they are free of all Jewish cultural laws and ritual prescriptions. Those who want them to observe these practices, Paul told them, are taking that position only to avoid persecution as servants of the Cross of Christ. His own conviction, he tells them at the beginning of this reading, is that, instead of concealing his discipleship of Christ's Cross, he wants to boast of that Cross. But the Cross was a sign of shame, and Paul knew the Galatians would have a hard time accepting that statement. So he makes the point that what God really wants is, not observance of Jewish rites, but rather that they be "created anew" — then they would be able to grasp what he is saying. In other words, they must be "born again" through baptism.

Most of us have been baptized as infants, and so we have missed out on the thrilling experience to which Paul is referring. The Galatians would well remember the ritual of their baptism — first of all, their public affirmation of their faith in Jesus, followed by their going down naked into the baptismal waters while the sacramental words were loudly proclaimed over them, and, on their emergence, feeling the oil of the Holy Spirit's anointing being poured over their bodies, then being clothed with white garments and led before the congregation, standing with lighted candles in their hands, singing hymns. Catechists compared the bath of baptism to a mother's womb — sometimes it was actually built in the shape of a womb — to teach them that they were indeed becoming a 'new creation.'

If the Galatians could claim the power of the Spirit, Paul is saying, that had made them into God's new creation, then they should not shrink from the Cross, in which they would find power and new life. He reflects on his own bodily wounds that connect him to the power of the Cross and says, "I bear the brand marks of Jesus in my body." With these words, he expresses the realization that the Cross of Christ is not just something outside of him — it is a power and an energy within that sustains him.

Briefly, today's Gospel is a summary of Jesus' missionary

method, as he sent out his disciples to prepare the people for his own future visits. There were to be no 'lone rangers' on Jesus' team — they were to travel in pairs, taking nothing extra, relying upon the people to take care of their needs. There was to be no time wasted on idle chat with those they encountered along the way. Nor should people in the villages have to prepare a list of households that would entertain them — they were to stay in one place, healing the sick and announcing the Kingdom of God. A severe warning was to be given to any town that did not welcome them. Jesus' missionary method, and his team of seventy-two witnesses, raises a question for us: What is our method of evangelization as a Christian community? Do we have a plan for offering the Gospel to others, or do we simply depend on people's inquiries to provide our church with new members? What can we learn from Jesus' directives?

A feast of God's word is provided for us each weekend, but often we only nibble at the nourishment offered. In a few moments, we will share in a second feast, that of the Lord's Eucharist. Let's see what we can do to continue savoring this marvelous nourishment of word and sacrament throughout the coming week, and witnessing to its flavor by the love and truth we share with others.

FIFTEENTH SUNDAY IN ORDINARY TIME
Dt 30:10-14   Col 1:15-20   Lk 10:25-37

The story of the Good Samaritan is a powerful attack on racial, nationalistic and religious prejudices

The question, "Who is my neighbor?" is as relevant and challenging a question today as it was in the time of Jesus. Tribalism, nationalism, religious prejudices, ancient rivalries between societies and the rampant greed of the global market all contribute in our own times to the denial of what Jesus was teaching in the parable of the Good Samaritan — that we are all neighbors. The Second Vatican Council taught that it is God's will that all people should form one family.[1] It's a lesson that most people, even Christians, don't seem to have yet learnt.

Let's reflect on this story for a moment. It's clear that Jesus chose his characters carefully, with the intention of making a number of points. First of all, the man who fell prey to robbers was obviously a Jew. The priest and Levite, or Temple assistant, were leaders of the Jewish community. The Samaritan was a member of a community that Jews were taught to despise. Centuries before, the Samaritans' Jewish ancestors, after many of their own people had been carried off into exile in Babylon, had started intermarrying with foreigners because of a shortage of women of marriageable age. When the Jews returned from Babylon fifty years later, they cut the Samaritans off and would have nothing to do with them. They were looked upon as law-breakers — people of mixed race — an unclean society of half-castes. The genuineness even of their Jewish faith was denied.

As he continued with the story, Jesus went into detail about the lengths to which this Samaritan went to help the wounded man. He not only dressed his wounds and brought him to an inn, where he took care of him — he also paid the innkeeper to look after him while he continued on his journey. Then he even went further than that. He told the innkeeper that he would reimburse him for any extra expense on his return journey. Jesus then invited the lawyer to decide which of these three had been neighbor to the wounded man. I'm sure the lawyer must have felt some reluctance to do that. Remember, at the beginning of this account, when the lawyer had asked Jesus "Who is my neighbor?", we're told that he asked it "because he wished to justify himself." The reason for that remark is that the text from the Book of Leviticus that Jesus had quoted about loving one's neighbor had always been interpreted by the lawyers as referring only to fellow-Jews. The purpose of asking the question, "Who is my neighbor?" was to pressure Jesus into supporting that interpretation. But now the ploy had backfired, and he was in a very uncomfortable position. He would have looked very foolish if he had claimed that the Jewish priest or the Levite had acted like neighbors to the injured man.

Jesus than got the reply he wanted. The point of the story was so obvious and so powerfully made that this Jewish lawyer — an expert in the Law — was forced to swallow his own wisdom and ignore the official interpretation of that Law. He was forced to ignore the age-old ban on relationships with Samaritans and acknowledge that the only person in the story who actually deserved the name of 'neighbor' to the Jew who had fallen among robbers was the despised Samaritan. Jesus had the final word. He then told the lawyer to go and be a 'good Samaritan' himself!

This story represents a powerful attack on racial, nationalistic and religious prejudices. The despised and rejected Samaritan turns out to be a deeply human, compassionate person. The details in the story about the Samaritan's generosity to his traditional enemy, a Jew, are a total refutation and condemnation of the blind prejudice of people of that time, and of people today. "Go and do the same" is addressed to us too.

---

[1] *The Church in the Modern World*, # 24.

ASSUMPTION OF MARY

Rv 11:19a, 12:1-6a   1 Cor 15:20-27   Lk 1:39-56

Mary's feasts symbolize and express in a certain way
the vocation of all Christians

Since the Second Vatican Council, the Church is more conscious of the fact that Mary's dignity does not separate her from the rest of its believing members. During the Council, there were a number of bishops who wanted a special teaching document about Mary to be issued. This proposal was debated by the assembly, and voted down. The view that prevailed was that Mary not be presented as a privileged person whose special privileges separate her from, and exalt her above, the rest of the Church. Rather, she was to be seen by all as a member of the Church, the first of those to be redeemed by the sacrifice of her Son. Therefore the Council fathers decided, rather than producing a separate document on Mary, to insert a teaching about her into their document on the Church, which then became its eighth chapter.

In line with that development, the celebrations of Mary's feasts are preferably to be seen and celebrated, not simply as recognitions of her favored position, but as events that symbolize and express in a certain way the vocation of all Christians. For example, Mary's immaculate conception is a sign pointing to the task of all Christians to shake off the shackles of sin and live the new life we have been given in baptism. Her visit to Elizabeth is a call to us to be aware of what God is doing in our lives and to give thanks for the blessings we have received. Mary's giving birth to her Son is a figure of the task of every Christian — to bring Jesus to birth again in the witness of his or her own life. Mary's standing by the Cross is a reminder that we too, if we want to grow spiritually, must also sometimes stand with her beside the Cross of her Son. Mary's Assumption into heaven, that we celebrate today, is a sign of our future destiny to join her and all the saints in eternal life.

Mary is also, in the Church's tradition, a model of what the

Church itself should be — full of faith and love, always united with Jesus her Son. Our task is to reproduce in the Church the qualities and virtues of Mary — her openness to God's will expressed in her obedience at the Incarnation, and her acceptance of the kind of life that decision would mean for her, with all its joys and sufferings. Mary would have had no idea of the controversy that would swirl about her home in Nazareth once her Son's public life started. No doubt she also experienced, and had to accept, some of the hostility and rejection that was directed at him. The testing of her faith, and sometimes the sense of God's absence, was probably a frequent experience during that time. The Church's faith today is likewise being tested amid the controversies and sometimes the hostility of the world. Like Mary, it has to anchor itself too in faithful obedience to God's word.

Another aspect of the Church's constant teaching about Mary is that devotion to Mary must never be an end in itself — it must always lead us to her Son. Reflection on the courage and faithfulness of Mary reminds us that it was the result of a very powerful experience of God. The celebration of her feast is an invitation to each one of us to open our hearts to the Lord, as she did. There's also a promise contained there that the blessings that have come to the Church through Mary's faithful obedience are meant for us too.

SIXTEENTH SUNDAY IN ORDINARY TIME

Gn 18:1-10a   Col 1:24-28   Lk 10:38-42

What Martha experienced is a pattern or model of the usual process of spiritual growth for most of us

We live in an action-oriented culture that glorifies achievers and doers. We praise people who are known as 'movers and shakers' or someone who "really gets things done." If somebody seems to spend too much time talking about a problem, he or she is likely to be told, "Get off your duff and do something about it." Our culture is suspicious of people who have a preference for thinking and reflecting and listening. For example, we say something is 'merely academic.' meaning it has no importance in the so-called real world, and we refer to professorial types as 'egg-heads' — not exactly a complimentary description. Yes, we live in an action and achievement-oriented culture.

What then are we to make of this story in today's Gospel, where the mover and shaker in the kitchen is rebuked, and the one who quietly sits and listens and reflects is praised? First of all, we need to put the story in context. It comes immediately after the story of the Good Samaritan, that we heard last Sunday. You remember the punch-line in that story was, "Go and do likewise," that is, 'Be a good Samaritan yourself!' The story we heard today has been placed here probably to balance that advice with a reminder that there's something else that's important too. Jesus is not simply praising the reflective person and putting down the person of action.

But that's not all. There's a profound depth to many of the Gospel stories, and this one is an example of that. It's much more than a comparison between two attitudes, reflective versus active. Maybe commentators and preachers in the past have focused too much on Mary. I say this because there is also much to be learnt from Martha's experience. That is because what she experienced is actually a pattern or model of the usual process of spiritual growth for most of us. Mary's way is certainly the better way, but hers represents a special calling — to remain before the Lord in contemplation. But when Jesus said that Mary's was the "better" part, he was recognizing that Martha's way was also good. He was not inviting her to sit at his feet too and let everyone go hungry. Martha working in the kitchen is a model for most of us who are active in our day-to-day lives and perhaps in some form of Christian service too. There's a 'Martha' in most of us, so we can easily identify with her and sympathize with her experience. No doubt there was a lot of darkness in that kitchen when Martha returned to it after the Lord's response. She was doing what she was doing out of love for him, but, instead of some sympathy for her burdens in the kitchen, she got rebuked!

If we think about it, Martha's experience of darkness, despite her best intentions, is not unfamiliar to many people. For example, there are people who, in one way or another, give themselves generously to some worthwhile project, either in the church or elsewhere, but find themselves not appreciated, or even criticized or rejected. Most of us, at one time or another, have come up against people who are narrow-minded, overly critical, or blind to the needs that we clearly see. Their criticism or rejection can bring darkness into our lives. We can get very angry with those kind of people, when we think of the good things they are obstructing. We may even see them as interfering with the Lord's work.

But there is another way of looking at the situation. Suppose the Lord has allowed this frustration and rejection to happen to us because he wants to bring us closer to himself? Maybe what we are doing is what *we* think the Lord expects of us, but that may not actually be the case. The fact is that most of us tend to take the Lord for granted when things are going well. It's only in hard times that he becomes more real to us. Out of our darkness may come the realization that the Lord may not see things the same way as we do, and that some kind of 'failure' or rejection may play an important role in bringing us closer to him. We need to recall over and over again that the message of the Cross is one of victory through failure. In the midst of failure, or rejection of our efforts, is found the invitation to true poverty of spirit, that is, a letting-go of our own wishes and a deeper openness to what God may be asking of us.[1] That was the lesson Martha had to learn in her kitchen that day. It's a lesson for us too.

---

[1] The inspiration for this homily comes from Thomas H. Green, SJ, *Darkness in the Market Place* (Notre Dame, Indiana: Ave Maria Press), 1981, pp 25-53.

SEVENTEENTH SUNDAY IN ORDINARY TIME
Gn 18:20-32   Col 2:12-14   Lk 11:1-13

Biblical images invite us to get acquainted and involved with God

Most of us have, on occasion, been affected by another person's prejudices. We meet someone for the first time, for example, but we already have an image of what that person is like because of what we have heard about him or her. Such prejudices can influence our whole way of relating to a person, or they may prevent us from relating at all. In the same way, our image of God, whether positive or negative, can also have a strong influence on how we relate to God and on how we pray.

In today's first reading we are presented with a fascinating, and rather amusing image of God: Yahweh seems to be running a Near-Eastern bazaar, and Abraham is haggling with him over the price he is charging. Although the metaphor is transferred to the issue of God's punishment of Sodom, the action is very much that of the market place. Abraham does an excellent job of beating Yahweh down on the price, and in the end, Sodom will be saved if only ten just people are found in it. It's a striking example of the interface between culture and religion, and how effective a culturally-generated image can be in communicating religious values. At the same time, it's a rather benign image of a God who is ready to cut a generous deal with Abraham. Yahweh's image in this story is that of a God who is prepared to do business with any reasonable person!

But that is only one of a number of images of God that we find throughout the Bible. In Genesis, chapter eighteen, we find the God who appears as a stranger to Abraham as he sits at the entrance to his tent in the heat of the day. Abraham makes him welcome and offers refreshment, food and rest. The grateful God, still in the guise of a stranger, accepts, and, upon making his departure, tells Abraham that the elderly Sarah will bear a child within a year. Sarah overhears this from inside the tent, and laughs at such apparent nonsense, but when she is confronted about it, she becomes afraid and says, "I didn't laugh." But the stranger insists, "Yes, you did." What a marvelous, down to earth image of a God who wants to be part of people's lives — a God who confronts doubters and who rewards handsomely those who accept him! This story reminds us too of what Jesus later said — that a welcome offered to disciples would also be a welcome to himself.

In the thirty-second chapter of Genesis, we have another surprising image of God. God is pictured as a wrestler, in fact, a wrestler who is unable to defeat Jacob, his opponent. Jacob's hip socket is wrenched during the contest, and he is left with a limp, but he refuses to release the divine being who is contending with him until he blesses him. The image of a God who wounds and blesses at the same time is a striking symbol of the spiritual journey that we're all called to make — a journey where it is often through the experience of wounding and darkness that we also experience God's presence and blessing.

In the Book of Isaiah, God is the mother who does not forget her child, and, in the New Testament, God is a hen who gathers her chicks under her wings. There are many other images throughout the Bible, such as shepherd, judge, father, creator. God is also the good housewife who sweeps the house carefully until, rejoicing, she has found the lost coin; the generous vineyard owner who hires unemployed piece-workers even late in the day; and the great lover of humanity who dies on a Cross.

As we reflect on Jesus' words in the Gospel about persisting in prayer, we know we can bring to it the richness of a long biblical tradition of colorful images that communicate something of the great diversity of God, God's adaptability to our human situation, and God's immense longing to be involved with us. These images invite us to get acquainted and involved with God. They also give promise of a rewarding and even exciting relationship.

EIGHTEENTH SUNDAY IN ORDINARY TIME
Ec 1:2, 2:21-23   Col 3:1-5, 9-11   Lk 12:13-21

Are we fools by the standards of the Gospel?

Many people dream of winning the lottery — of suddenly having lots of money, a better sense of security and no more financial problems. They could then put their feet up and do a number of things they had always wanted to do — take some trips to faraway places, have nice parties for their friends and many other good things to enjoy. The man in today's Gospel must have had similar feelings. He had just hit the jackpot with a bumper harvest, and he's feeling very good about his future. There's security for years to come. He can relax, have a good time, eat and drink to his heart's content. But Jesus calls him a fool.

Just before he told this story, Jesus had said that a person's possessions do not guarantee him life, even when he is wealthy. Now he calls this man a fool, not because he doesn't know that he is about to die and leave everything he is carefully saving behind, but because he doesn't understand how to be secure in the eyes of God. He thinks security is about having more than enough for himself for years to come. If he hoards his goods in large barns, he believes, then he will be able to enjoy life with nothing to worry about.

Jesus' criticism of him centers on the fact that he has grown rich "for himself instead of growing rich in the sight of God." Clearly, the point at issue here is that the man has grown rich "for himself." In the succeeding verses in St. Luke's Gospel (unfortunately not quoted in today's reading), Jesus goes on to flesh out what he means. "Consider the ravens," he says, "they do not sow, they do not reap, they have neither cellar nor barn — yet God feeds them.... Stop worrying. [...] Seek out instead his kingship over you, and the rest will follow in turn." What Jesus is saying here is something very difficult for people to accept. A person might object, "It's all very well to trust in God, but that won't pay the bills!" Or someone might conclude that a person who wants to take these sayings seriously would have to join a religious community. Is it possible that that's what Jesus intended — that his beautiful words about the ravens and the lilies of the field and about trusting in God's providence should be ignored by most people, because they were only intended for an elite few? There is no evidence that that is the case. Luke quotes Jesus' words on another occasion, "Give, and it shall be given to you" (Lk 6:38). And there are many other sayings of Jesus, for example, "It is more blessed to give than to receive" (Ac 20:35), that make it clear that hoarding up wealth is contrary to the spirit of the Gospel. For Jesus, the person who is blessed and happy is the one who is more interested in giving away than in receiving, who is ready to let go rather than hold onto things. That ability only comes from trust in God. What all this amounts to is that the Gospel is calling faithful followers of Jesus to live a simple life.

Of course our culture will always give us a different message. Cultural wisdom assures us that happiness and security will follow on taking good care of ourselves and making ample plans for our future. Popular culture invites us to center our lives on ourselves and our own concerns, but the Gospel, on the contrary, demands that we center our lives on others. Is that an impossible ideal? Not at all — in fact, good parents show us the way. The Gospel ideal is lived out, with great love, by many people who sacrifice themselves for their children, and often for their elderly parents too. When that kind of self-giving love extends itself generously to others as well, the spirit of the Gospel is there. Jesus expressed this by telling us to "seek first" (Mt 6:33) the Father's kingship, "and the rest will follow in turn." By these words, the Lord is inviting his disciples, and ourselves, to establish some priorities in our lives — priorities that may differ from those we now have. He is promising us that, if we pursue whole-heartedly the values of the Kingdom, especially in sharing gener-ously what we have, in giving away what we don't need, in demand-ing justice for the poor and the powerless, then, what we need to live off will never be lacking to us.

Jesus' strong condemnation of the man who had the rich har-vest, and his self-centered plans for himself, must give pause to all of us. It raises a question — a question only we ourselves can answer. Are we fools by the standards of the Gospel? Are we possibly in the same situation as the fool in this story? And, if so, what are we willing to do about it?

Faith is much more than a mental conviction that God exists

Faith is a critical issue in our modern world. Many people don't have any faith — they see it as outdated and outmoded. Others give only lip service to it. They see religion as performing a valuable role in society in terms of inculcating basic human values, but recognize little beyond that. Others, whether politicians, business people or so-called 'religious practitioners' manipulate religion for their own ends. If we reflect on society at large today, there seems to be a tremendous gap between faith, on the one hand, and the actual practice of Gospel values on the other.

The second reading we just heard, about the faith of Abraham, Sarah and their descendants, focuses our attention on the issue of faith. What kind of faith do *we* have? How real is it? Is it strong or weak? Some people's faith remains immature all their lives. It may be because it's just 'group faith' — that is, the faith of a person who accepts without question the beliefs of the social group to which he or she belongs, without any serious reflection on its meaning. Such a person might go to live in a foreign country that had a different religion, and have no problem switching to it, because his or her faith is like a coat that may be put on or taken off at will. It's mostly a matter of social convenience, having little to do with the values that are expressed in daily life.

Other people's faith is immature because they have a childish image of God. For them, God is an old man in the sky who rewards those who do good and punishes those who do wrong. So what happens when bad things happen to good people? There's a crisis, because they're not able to handle that. They believe that if they do what's right, God should take care of them. Such people may lose their faith in God because of some tragedy, for example, the loss of a child. They seem to think that God owes them something. But real faith has to go deeper than that.

What then is real faith? It's much more than a mental conviction that there is a God who exists. For people of our age, it brings with it an awareness of the inner presence of a creative God unfolding in the universe for the past fifteen billion years, and, in our age, developing into a dynamic relationship between a loving God and humanity.[1] Faith is our response to the experience of God's presence — in the emerging universe, in the bountiful earth, in the events of our lives, in our interactions with people and especially in Jesus Christ, the living revelation of God. Faith is an active listening to the voice of God resounding forth from the earth he has created. It is like standing with Moses at the Burning Bush, except that the whole of creation is now our Burning Bush. Genuine faith involves a relationship with God — an ongoing relationship of trust and dependence that includes trust in the goodness of everything he has created and is creating.

Jesus once said, "Come to me, all you who labor and are burdened." He invited people to entrust their lives to him. It's like a bond between two friends who can trust and rely on each other completely. Real friendship doesn't happen instantly between people — it has to be tested. Often there are ups and downs in friendship, and people have to work at it to make it a success. Our relationship with God will be the same. It will require struggling sometimes with doubts and difficulties — with a mystery that we can't fully understand. It may even mean that we sometimes get angry with God. Eventually we will come to realize that, though there may continue to be problems and losses and sufferings in our lives, and God may not take them away, still, he remains with us through the dark times. Even when he seems to be absent, God will always be there to support us, so that our faith will not be tested beyond endurance.

Returning to Abraham's relationship with God, we see that having genuine faith, and responding to its call, meant for him that he could no longer stay in the place where he had grown up. He left his own country and people, and journeyed to a distant land. For us too, our faith is not a gift we put away in a box — it constantly invites us to action. Abraham's journey challenges us to ask ourselves:

Is our faith moving us forward? Has it raised our consciousness of God's presence and God's call, has it given us a vision and a direction in our life? Or is it only an hour in church on weekends that has little or no connection with the rest of our week?

---

[1] See Cletus Wessels, *Jesus in the New Universe Story* (Orbis Books: Maryknoll, New York, 2003), pp. 66ff.

TWENTIETH SUNDAY IN ORDINARY TIME
Jr 38:4-6, 8-10   Heb 12:1-4   Lk 12:49-53

Conflict and opposition can play an important role
in our spiritual growth

Many people have heard the expression 'creative conflict.' But even if we have, most of us tend to regard conflict as a bad, stressful thing — something to be avoided. Yet, in the Gospel reading we just heard, Jesus seems to be welcoming conflict, even family conflict! He came, he says, to cast fire on the earth, and he is anxious to see that fire blaze up. But how does this statement compare with the angels' message about peace at Jesus' birth? Of course, there was Simeon's prophecy, addressed to Mary, that Jesus would be a sign that would be opposed, and that a sword would pierce her own heart. It would seem that Jesus' message would bring inner peace to those who could take it in, but it would also bring conflict and division in their day to day life.

Is there a contradiction here? Can inner peace and outer conflict go hand in hand in the life of a person? Certainly it can, when one looks at the matter from the point of view of Christian disciple-ship and the life of the Spirit. The sixteenth century contemplative saint, John of the Cross, for example, was involved in tremendous controversy and conflict in his efforts to reform his religious Order. His work was strongly opposed by many of his brothers. He was even imprisoned by some of them, locked up in a small cell and whipped several times a week in an effort to get him to change direction and admit that he had been in error. But he was at peace with the measures he had taken. And it was the darkness of his life during that period that provided him with the inspiration to begin his famous writing on spiritual darkness. The fact is that conflict and the things that often accompany it, such as accusations, opposition, misunder-standings, criticism and rejection, can play an important role in our spiritual growth.

But what is growing spiritually actually all about? It may be described as a process of surrendering our lives into the hands of

God. That doesn't happen without an inner struggle, because most of us like to keep control of our lives. It's our periods of darkness — times of failure or loss, or times when we experience opposition, for example, that can be opportunities for this kind of spiritual growth to take place. Instead of our usual way of responding, we could choose to throw ourselves into the arms of God, and ask the Lord where he wishes to lead us. It's during such painful times that we are confronted with the reality of our spiritual poverty, and with the blindness of relying on ourselves and our own way of seeing things. We can come to realize that we need to learn anew the way of the Lord. It's a process of purification that will help us focus on the Lord more intently. It's a time of enlightenment, when we come to see that we've been taking God for granted, and that there's a fascinating mystery at the heart of our life of faith that we have never really allowed to come close to us. We will find ourselves wanting to experience God. The images of God that have satisfied us up to now will no longer be enough, and we will start looking for a more satisfying way to pray.

To return to today's Gospel — what Jesus is looking forward to is the beginning of that deepening process that will soon begin for his disciples. The darkness of conflict and opposition is coming. They may even lose close family ties that are very important to them, and other relationships they have come to rely upon. Instead of taking the Good News for granted, they will need to open their hearts totally, and experience it as the power of God in their lives. They will come to see their problems in a new way. They will gradually become aware that God is doing something new in them, and that they will have to let go of their own fixed expectations and allow the Lord to lead them.

Some of us may hear in these words the invitation to say 'yes' to the Lord's work within us. It's a purifying process that can be painful at times. We may hesitate to embark on it. We have fears about entering a world that we don't understand, and about being blindly led on the journey when we're not sure where it may lead. But the invitation is always there, and the blessings are unlimited.

God's will for the human race is unity

The first reading we just heard, from the prophet Isaiah, begins with the words, "I am coming to gather together the nations of every language." In the Gospel, Jesus tells us that people from east and west, north and south, will come to take their places at the feast in the Kingdom of God. What the Scriptures are saying is that it is God's strong desire to bring people together. Unity is one of the signs of the Gospel's presence, and it's a sign of the presence of disciples of Jesus.

But the reality for most of us is that we don't experience much unity. In fact, we're much more likely to experience separateness, division, fragmentation and violence in our world today. Many people are alienated — they don't feel connected to others. We're divided by color, ethnicity, religion, levels of education and wealth, and different cultural attitudes. All of these things give rise to prejudice, and there's plenty of that too. But the call and challenge of the Gospel is to change our attitudes — to take part in bringing God's reign into our world by working for unity and establishing God's universal family.

Where might we begin that task? First of all, we must allow ourselves to feel the painfulness of the situation in our world today. Some people never reflect on what is going on around them from day to day — they never reach any real level of awareness that would motivate them to try to create a better world. They just take it all for granted. Their main concerns remain for the most part at the animal level of eating, drinking and mating. If they come to church and listen to the Gospel, it seems to pass over their heads, and they go through the week as if they had never heard it. But the Scripture is proclaimed in our hearing so that we can do something about it — it challenges us to take God seriously. Today's Scripture invites us to hear the message that God's will for the human race is unity. If we're willing to hear that message and think about it, then we cannot but be disturbed by the disunity and separateness that is a common experience today. And being disturbed by those things should move us towards doing something about them. But what can we do? We all sometimes feel helpless about the larger problems we see around us. Yet even a small ripple in the center of a lake can spread out as far as the shore.

My first suggestion has to do with reconciliation. Reconciliation happens when people are willing to put aside their prejudices and come closer together. Each one of us should be convinced that we must reach out with a welcome to people, including those who are different from ourselves. We'll never understand what God's Kingdom is all about as long as we're willing only to recognize those who are like ourselves. The power of the Gospel, if we're open to it, is a driving force urging us to bring people together. We should make it a personal priority to make friends with people who are of a different ethnic, cultural or religious background from ourselves. That is what bringing in the Kingdom is all about, and that is what experiencing the presence of the Kingdom is all about. We also may need reconciliation within ourselves. Many people have no inner peace because they're constantly being pulled this way and that by their fears or their angers or jealousies. We can resolve to let go of these things if we want to, and invite the Spirit to come and bring us peace of heart.

The second point is about healing. The Gospels are full of healing stories. Healing people was one of the ways Jesus used for announcing that the power of evil was being overcome and that the Kingdom of God was breaking into the world. People who were healed usually came to a change of faith and a new heart. Today the need for healing is all around us. The world is full of emotional pain. Our young people are growing up experiencing many things that hurt them — parental divorce, loneliness, violence, sexual abuse, the absence of love. We need to have more healing services in our Catholic communities — people should not have to go to other churches for healing. Neighborhoods too can find healing through anti-drug and anti-violence programs, for example. Wherever there is healing, there is the Kingdom of God.

The final point has to do with liberation. Although we claim to live in a free country, many people are not inwardly free. They have little self-discipline, they're slaves to their passions and desires, they're driven by whatever feeling urges them on at any given moment. St. Paul tells us that Jesus has freed us from the law of sin and death. Freedom, just like reconciliation and healing, must come from within ourselves. To become inwardly free is a process. It involves a deep personal transformation, and the opening up of a person to the power of God's Spirit. It involves a surrender and a letting-go of the things that enslave us, followed by a movement in a different direction.

I began this homily by talking about God's great desire to bring all people together, and how this is actually what the Kingdom of God is all about. The holy meal we are about to share together is a reminder of what this unity means. When we celebrate the Eucharist, we are making the Kingdom of God symbolically present. It will be up to us then to make it a reality in our daily lives.

TWENTY-SECOND SUNDAY IN ORDINARY TIME
Si 3:17-18, 20, 28-29   Heb 12:18-19, 22-24a   Lk 14:1, 7-14

In this parable, Jesus is trying to move us beyond self-centeredness

Each time the Olympic Games come round, they give us examples of how far some participants will go in order to get to the top, even risking disgrace and the termination of their careers by taking drugs. Closer to home, it's also clear that people will make big sacrifices in order to be first — to have the most spectacular party, the finest clothes, the sportiest car, etc. — just for the feeling that they're a step ahead of everyone else.

In today's Gospel, Jesus takes note of this common human weakness. He observes people rushing forward to take the most honorable seats at a meal, and he doesn't approve of it. He comments, "Everyone who exalts himself shall be humbled...." On another occasion he warned people that the first would be last and the last first. Jesus seems to be making a basic point here about discipleship. He expects of his disciples that they should be willing to take the last place. Why? Probably because the desire to be first reveals a preoccupation with oneself. Self-centered discipleship is a contradiction in terms — disciples should look to their master. We're all therefore challenged by Jesus' words to move from a life that's centered on self to a life that's centered on God. How can we know if we're still centered on self, and how do we grow beyond self-centeredness? Studies have identified several stages in the process, as a person moves from one kind of motivation for action to another. Reflecting on them should help us identify where we are on this journey:

The first and most basic stage — the stage of a small child — is when a person is motivated simply by desire for reward or fear of punishment. In other words, if there's a reward to be gained, or if I might suffer some loss, I'll make the extra effort to do something that I would not otherwise do. Many people remain fixated at this level their whole lives. They're always asking, "What's in it for me?"

The second stage may be described by the expression, "I'll scratch your back if you scratch mine" — in other words, I am willing to help you now, because I'm hoping to get you to do a favor for me later. I'm sure many of us have come across people who are at this stage. They willingly do us a favor, but later on we find that there is a price to pay.

I have arrived at the third stage when I am willing to make a sacrifice or take a risk in order to help someone, but only because I know people will notice what I am doing, and will be impressed by what a wonderful person I am! Popularity is the goal at this stage.

At any of these three stages, a person's behavior is still centered on self. He or she may do what is morally right, but motivation springs from individual needs, and not from any desire to reach out to others.

The fourth stage is known as the 'law and order' stage. If something is the law, that I should report an accident, for example, then I'll do the conventional thing and report it. Most people never go beyond this stage. They're willing to observe the everyday rules of society, but not do anything over and above.

It's only at the fifth stage, however, that a person begins to reach out beyond preoccupation with self and becomes capable of approaching the values of the Gospel. This is where I recognize that I am part of a community, and I am willing to share in community responsibilities, for example, by participating in cleaning up a park, or raising funds for an orphanage, even though I may not directly benefit from the project.

It's only when I arrive at the sixth stage that I am able to recognize, after reflection, that we're all God's precious children, and so, I'm willing to spend myself in trying to bring in the Kingdom of God and his justice, even though I may suffer some loss. By doing that, God's love and compassion will take stronger root in my heart, and I am content simply with knowing that. I don't need any other reward.

The fact that I am familiar with these stages does not, of course, mean that I have grown through them. For that to begin to happen, the values they contain must move from head to heart, especially when it comes to the last two stages. When I allow myself to feel compassion for others, then preoccupation with self will fall away. I will be willing, as Jesus advises, to take the last place.

TWENTY-THIRD SUNDAY IN ORDINARY TIME

Ws 9:13-18b   Phm 9-10, 12-17   Lk 14:25-33

*The Gospel concerns not only a person's relationship
with God and neighbor; it also has implications for the kind of
society we should be building*

Sometimes, when we look in the pages of the New Testament for a text that will support the condemnation of certain things we regard as wrong, we come away disappointed. People have looked, for example, for a clear statement condemning the subject status of women in the ancient world. Others have searched there in vain for a condemnation of slavery. Efforts to account for these absences have ranged from comments on the different cultural attitudes of biblical writers to conclusions that the New Testament approved of some things that we strongly disapprove of today. The correct answer, however, is somewhere in the middle.

If we read the Gospels carefully, for example, we will discover that Jesus had a very different attitude towards women than his contemporaries. When it comes to slavery, while it is true that there is no outright condemnation of it, there is certainly the beginnings of a change of attitude. This change may be seen in the second reading for today, from Paul's Letter to Philemon.

This letter is a personal, private message from Paul to his friend Philemon. It was obviously seen by the early Christians as having wider importance for the Church, and so, has been received into the Scriptures. Onesimus was Philemon's slave who had run away from his owner, and had probably stolen something also while escaping. He had come to Paul in Rome, who had instructed and baptized him. Paul says in the letter that he would have liked to have kept Onesimus with him in Rome, but he was not willing to do that without Philemon's permission. So he is sending the runaway slave back to him. This must have been a frightening proposal for Onesimus. Philemon could have him executed for running away. But Paul writes this letter to ask Philemon to take him back. However, he asks him to take him back, not as a slave any longer, but as a fellow-disciple of the Lord, and therefore a brother. That seems to be what eventually happened, since Philemon must have published this letter within the Christian community, which preserved it. This is the only place in the New Testament where there is an implied rejection of slavery, at least for Christians. Paul is telling Philemon, "Now that I have baptized him, he is your brother — so don't make a slave of him again."

For centuries people have privatized the Gospel, and have interpreted it as having to do with a person's individual relationship with God. However, we can see here, in the reception of Paul's letter into the New Testament, the beginnings of a reflective awareness that the Gospel does have implications for society in general, and that its spirit will inevitably lead to social criticism. That awareness in the Church has continued through the centuries right up to the present, and has become sharper in recent times, in particular with regard to three issues:

A number of years ago Cardinal Bernardin of Chicago pointed out that Christians, to be consistent in their defense of the sacredness of life, must defend human life at all its stages and in all circumstances. He used the analogy of Jesus' seamless garment, that could not to be divided. The cardinal's view has since become part of the Church's official teaching. That is why, for example, Catholics cannot support the death penalty except in very exceptional circumstances.

The 'just war' theory of St. Thomas Aquinas, that laid down several conditions for waging a just war, has had a strong influence on the Church's teaching about war for seven hundred years. However, St. Thomas knew nothing about weapons of mass destruction. Our late Holy Father, Pope John Paul II taught that war may no longer be regarded as a fitting instrument for resolving conflicts between nations. In fact, looking at the situation in the world today, it is getting more and more difficult to see how any war, except one that is purely defensive, may be considered just.

A third point has to do with economic issues. For over one

hundred years, the Church has taken a strong stand on justice for working people. For example, employment may not be seen simply as a function of the so-called 'Free Market' and of the profits derived from it. It is the natural right of each person, as is also a living wage that will support their families. These rights cannot simply be left to the mercy of market forces, and governments have a moral responsibility to see to it that that does not happen.

So, as we reflect today on Paul's compassionate Letter to Philemon and its broader implications for society of that time, we can come to realize that the teachings of Jesus concern, not only how we should live as individuals and how we should behave in our private lives and personal relationships, but also the kind of just society we should be trying to build up.

The old man who loves us to the point of foolishness is none other than God our Father

The story of the prodigal son is perhaps the best-known of all the stories that Jesus told. It's a universal story, for all times and cultures. After two thousand years, it hasn't lost any of its power, because it speaks to a universal human experience — the relationship between parents and their children, the rebellion of young people against the authority of their parents, and the reconciliation that is needed within all families from time to time. What this story is ultimately about, of course, is the relationship between God and ourselves.

Let's look at the details for a moment. The younger son said to his father, "Give me my share of the inheritance." He couldn't wait for his father to die off. He was anxious to get away from home, where he could be totally free from any parental control — where he could have money in his pocket and do whatever he wished without anybody looking over his shoulder. He thought everything would be fine if he could just get away. His father didn't complain — he just did what his son asked of him. I'm sure the people listening to the story must have thought to themselves, "What a foolish old man!"

At any rate, his son went off to a foreign country and had a good time, with plenty of fair-weather friends, as long as his money lasted. But when famine came, they abandoned him, and he was forced to take a job feeding pigs. We must bear in mind that Jews are forbidden to have anything to do with pigs — they associated them with demons. Jesus is telling us just how low his selfishness and self-indulgence had brought the prodigal son. He had degraded himself to the lowest level. The good times had not brought him any real happiness. Finally we're told, he came to his senses. He began to see the reality of his situation — that he had been blind to his father's love, that he had misunderstood the meaning of freedom, that he had been looking for happiness in the wrong places, and he set off on his journey back to his father's house.

His father had never forgotten him — had never stopped loving him, in spite of what he had done. He went out scanning the horizon for him every day, until one day he saw him coming up the road. We're told that he ran out to meet him, threw his arms around his neck and kissed him. There's something else we need to take note of here. Older men in Jewish society were patriarchal figures. They moved about slowly with great dignity. They didn't run — they waited for people to come to them. Again we can imagine the listening people saying to themselves, "What a foolish old man — making an ass of himself running out to welcome back such a son." But the father makes no complaint. There's no rebuke or punishment or "Didn't I warn you that this would happen" — there's only joy and celebration.

And that's the point of the whole story. The old man who loves us to the point of foolishness is none other than God our Father. We are all his lost children, and he's waiting to welcome us back home. This is a story about us — about our selfishness and self-indulgence — about the times we preferred to look good rather than do good. It's about our blindness to what's really important — and it's about God our Father who is scanning the horizon every day with great love to see if we will finally come to our senses.

TWENTY-FIFTH SUNDAY IN ORDINARY TIME
Am 8:4-7   1 Tm 2:1-8   Lk 16:1-13

Are we children of the light, or are we children of this world?

Power, wealth and success are held in high regard around the world. People who have been successful with money, whether in the stock market, property deals or in business, get a lot of respect. We hear that such-and-such a person 'is worth' so many millions. That's an interesting expression — to be 'worth' a certain amount of money. It makes a point about where 'worth' and value are thought to be found, and in what kinds of things they consist. The major passion of many people is making money. They put a great deal of energy into acquiring it, and, having once acquired it, into holding onto it.

The Gospel constantly belittles that kind of success. There are, for example, the stories of the rich young man who wasn't willing to let go of his riches for the sake of the Kingdom, of the wealthy farmer congratulating himself on his bumper harvest and making plans to enjoy his accumulated wealth, but who doesn't know that he is going to die that very night; and the frightening story of the rich man and the hungry beggar Lazarus lying at his gate, covered with sores.

Today's Gospel tells us without equivocation, "You cannot give yourself to God and money." There's an ironic commendation of the wasteful steward who is very astute in providing dishonestly for his own future. The children of this world are wiser, we're told, when it comes to their own concerns, than the children of light. People tend to be half-hearted when it comes to spiritual wealth, but energetic when it comes to accumulating material things. Quite clearly, Jesus would like us to be the opposite — energetic when it comes to accumulating spiritual wealth, and less diligent when it comes to accumulating material things. The Gospel doesn't want the matter of spiritual growth to be merely a side issue in our lives.

The basic question with which this message confronts us is: Are we really children of the light, or are we children of this world? The criterion for judging this is very clear: the children of this world put more of their energy into accumulating wealth, and less into growing spiritually, while the children of the light do the opposite. This Gospel holds a mirror up before us. Its uncompromising language is the Lord's attempt to get us to put aside any illusions about our practice of religion and look at the reality.

What illusions? For example, Sunday worship is an excellent thing. Its drawback is that it can create the illusion that everything is alright with us spiritually — that we are actually children of the light. Ritual actions, singing, vestments, candles, flowers and all the paraphernalia of worship can lull us into imagining that this is what religion is about. But that would only be true when we can bring to God in our worship the content of our daily lives. The energy of our lives must synchronize with the energy of worship — otherwise what we are doing here has very little to do either with God or spiritual growth.

If we want to respond to this Gospel message, where might we start? Spiritual writers have always maintained that the starting point for spiritual awareness and growth is self-knowledge. That can be a painful place to start, because many of us are less than what we seem to be. Richness of spirit comes from such things as regular personal prayer, reflection on the Scriptures, and a deep love and concern for the poor, even to the point of sacrifice. We just heard, in the first reading, the prophet Amos' vigorous condemnation of those who rush out from their worship services in order to defraud the poor. We might, on reflection, find ourselves to be like the person at the banquet who was found to have no wedding garment and was thrown out. The children of this world fear bankruptcy, and do what they can to avoid it. The children of light fear spiritual bankruptcy, and insure themselves against it by becoming spiritually rich. They are willing to take an honest, though sometimes painful look at themselves, and to ask themselves risky questions, such as: What does God want me to do, and how can I surrender my life, and all I have, into his hands?

TWENTY-SIXTH SUNDAY IN ORDINARY TIME
Am 6:1a, 4-7   1 Tm 6:11-16   Lk 1:19-31

Jesus chose to associate his teaching about hell with
a particular kind of sin

There are still preachers around who give 'hell-fire and brimstone sermons,' though such is more rare than previously in our Church, I suspect. A few of us may have heard those kind of sermons in our youth. Occasionally, we might see a letter to the editor in our local Catholic newspaper complaining about the 'easy Gospel' being taught in many churches, and wondering about what has happened to those terrifying sermons, and whether or not the existence of hell is still something the Church teaches.

The Gospel reading we just heard is a terrifying sermon all by itself. It's a reminder that 'hell' is still a part of the Church's teaching. 'Going to hell' is still a real possibility. What does this teaching mean? Basically, the Church's doctrine about hell is a consequence of our belief in the doctrine of free will. That means that, because I am free, I can welcome the Lord into my life, and try to live by the teachings of the Gospel. I am also free to reject the truth that I recognize and exclude God's love from my life. What the doctrine of hell means is that God will respect the freedom he has given each of us. He will never force himself upon us, either in this world or in the next. If the way I have chosen to live my life is a rejection of the Gospel, and I die in this situation, I will find myself separated from God. What about 'the fires of hell'? We need to remember that fire in the Bible is a symbol of God's judgment, and the word 'fire' is used many times in the Scriptures in this symbolic way. Therefore it is not true to say that God burns people for ever in hell. Actually, we don't know anything about hell except that it is a state of separation from God. In that situation of separateness consists the suffering of hell, because God has made us ultimately for himself. There can be no happiness where the presence of God cannot be experienced. The Church does not teach that any person is actually in hell. It remains simply a terrible possibility because of our freedom to choose the kind of life we wish to live.

What is especially noteworthy in today's Gospel is that Jesus chose to associate his teaching about hell with a particular kind of sin. This wasn't a sexual sin, or a crime of violence. The sin is neglect of the poor — the refusal to have compassion for a poor person who is in need, and is asking for help. Nor is the Lord referring here just to one incident. He is clearly referring to an attitude — an ongoing uncaring, uncompassionate attitude towards poor people. The same point is made in the account of the Last Judgment, in the twenty-fifth chapter of St. Matthew, where condemnation is earned because of people's uncaring attitude towards those who were hungry, thirsty, naked, strangers, sick people and prisoners.

We live in a society that is noteworthy for its frequent neglect of, and harshness towards, the poor. Perhaps we're still too much influenced by Calvinist theology and television preachers who would see prosperity as God's way of rewarding good people, ourselves among them. Society, in its official attitudes, laws and regulations, makes harsh judgments about people who cannot find work, who have children out of wedlock, or who have problems supporting their families on a very basic income. We read horror stories in the newspapers about poor people in desperate situations who are sent away from hospital emergency rooms because they have no insurance. How many poor people are languishing in prison simply because they can't afford a good lawyer? How many wealthy people end up on death row? We, of course, may wash our hands of responsibility, like Pilate — after all, what can we do? But we're part of this society, and therefore there's something of society's evils that sticks to all of us. Caring about the poor has to mean that we take the trouble to make ourselves aware of the factors in our society that oppress them, and that we actively protest against and oppose these factors. Injustice is not simply a matter of how one person treats another. Injustice towards the less fortunate today is organized and impersonal. It's often a matter of systemic inequality, structured into society. Disciples of Jesus Christ must also be organized in responding to injustice. We cannot listen to the warning message of this Gospel and ignore it.

TWENTY-SEVENTH SUNDAY IN ORDINARY TIME

Hab 1:2-3, 2:2-4   2 Tm 1:6-8, 13-14   Lk 17:5-10

On my faith-journey, God will share in my joys,
and God will suffer with me too

Both the first and third readings we just heard put the issue of faith before us. In the first reading, the prophet Habakkuk tells us that, in God's eyes, the just person will live because of his faith. In the Gospel, Jesus tells his disciples that even a little faith — faith the size of a mustard seed — can do great things. In our Catholic Church, the tradition of faith has, over the centuries, come to be identified in many people's minds with the content of faith — in other words, with the actual beliefs that we hold to be true. Teaching the faith has come to mean teaching the truths that the Church teaches, the teachings to be found in the catechism.

While these things are certainly important, it's also important to remember that faith is much more than knowledge. When Jesus invited people to have faith, he didn't take a catechism out of his pocket and hand it to them. No, what he first of all tried to do was to invite people to have trust — to place their trust in God, to put themselves trustingly in God's hands. God was doing something new through Jesus, and they were being challenged to let go of their fears and preconceived ideas and surrender themselves to what God wanted to do.

That is still what the challenge of faith is all about. It takes us beyond simply believing in God — it calls us to let go of our need to control our lives. That doesn't mean that we passively just let things happen. It means, first of all, that we recognize that our lives are part of a bigger picture, and that we want to fit in with the Lord's plans for us. So we leave room for the Lord to guide us in the decisions of our lives, and in the events that happen to us. In other words, we pray for guidance before we make significant decisions. How can we know that the Lord is actually guiding us? We may need a spiritual guide to help us in discerning that, but one thing to bear in mind is that the Lord always speaks in peace. In difficult times, and in difficult decisions, if the Lord is present, we will, in spite of everything, have an inner peace that nothing can take away from us.

If we do that kind of praying, what will it actually mean for us? Does it mean that everything will now start going well? No, it doesn't mean that. What it means is that God will now be part of my life, part of my journey, in a new way. God will share in my joys, and God will suffer with me too. Whether things go well or badly, I'll never be alone. Some verses of Scripture will become more important to me, for example, those lines in the Book of Psalms that call God 'my rock' because I will experience God as a constant support that never crumbles or falters, or the message that God has written my name on the palm of his hand, and that he will never forget me.

As I begin to grow into a deeper faith, I will find myself worrying less about such things as having lots of money or possessions, or about what people think of me. I will become more occupied with the question: How can I play my part in bringing in God's Kingdom into the world? Such things as justice and compassion will become more important to me — no longer in the sense of "I want justice" or "I want to be treated with compassion." Instead, rather, I will begin to think of all those people who experience little compassion or justice in their lives. Those kinds of issues will begin to occupy my thoughts — I will find myself wanting to do something about them — to make a difference by the way I live out my life.

So, as we reflect upon this Gospel today, we ask the Lord to give us even a mustard seed of faith — a little genuine faith that can move us beyond mechanical religious practice to real, committed discipleship. This is the kind of faith, in other words, that will start us on a journey with him as our companion, with him as the rock we can depend on, with him to share our joys and our sufferings. Where will that journey lead us? He alone knows that, but we don't have to worry, because he will be with us at every stage, and at the end.

TWENTY-EIGHTH SUNDAY IN ORDINARY TIME
2 K 5:14-17   2 Tm 2:8-13   Lk 17:11-19

*We need to thank God for the totality of our life — its pains as well
as its joys, its failures as well as its successes*

As we reflect on this story about the ten lepers, and the fact that only
one of them returned to give thanks, we might be tempted to think
that the ungrateful ones did not deserve to be healed. Certainly, if
this story had been taken from Greek culture, it would surely have
had a vengeful ending, because the Greeks were accustomed to
portraying their gods in their own image. In that case, the nine ungrateful lepers would have awakened the next morning to find that
their leprosy had returned, and nobody would have felt much sympathy for them. But that's not how the story actually ended, because
we're dealing with a gracious God who gives his gifts freely — and
so, all are healed, grateful and ungrateful alike.

We may indeed be self-righteously critical of those nine ungrateful lepers. But if we're honest, we'll have to admit that we're
not very faithful ourselves when it comes to thanking God. One of
the reasons for this may be that, when we do take time to give thanks
to God, we probably limit our thanks to what we see as 'good' things.
But the fact is that we should be extending our thanks beyond that.
In reality, we are not always accurate in judging what is actually good
for us. We need a broader view of things — we need to realize that
God's blessings are not limited only to the things that we ourselves
judge to be 'good.' We should thank God for the totality of our lives
— its pains as well as its joys, its losses and failures as well as its
gains and successes. Why should we do that? It seems to me that
one of the signs of a mature Christian is that a person is able to look
at everything, absolutely everything that has happened in the course
of his or her life, and recognize even in the painful experiences God's
mysterious way of teaching us compassion, of bringing us closer to
himself, of weaning us away from what is destructive, and helping
us to set our hearts on the more important things.

You may have heard of a well-known novel written by a

Frenchman, Georges Bernanos, called *The Diary of a Country Priest*. It's a sad story about a priest who was assigned to a country parish in France during the 1920s, and remained there for the rest of his life. He was an outsider in the little village, and the book describes all the suspicion and distrust and lack of acceptance he continued to encounter over the course of a very difficult ministry. At the end of the story, when he is dying, he looks back with eyes of faith at the whole experience — at the years that he has spent among these unresponsive people, years that some might consider a waste — and says, surprisingly, "*toutes est grace*" — everything is grace, everything is grace. That's the kind of mature Christian attitude I'm talking about. We've arrived there when we come to the point that we can say in the face of all the things that have happened in the course of our lives — "everything is grace."

St. John Chrysostom was bishop of Constantinople (modern day Istanbul) in the fourth century. He was a great preacher, and shortly after he arrived in the city from Antioch he began fearlessly to preach against the luxurious lifestyle of the emperor's household and local church officials. They turned on him with great hate, but he persisted. They then started to persecute him. People spread rumors that he was having all-night parties in the bishop's house, and that he was romantically involved with a certain widow. He was accused of selling off the precious vestments and chalices of the church, which was true, because he had indeed sold many of them to feed the poor during a time of famine. In the end, he was exiled by the emperor from Constantinople — temporarily at first — but eventually, when he would continue to persist after his return in preaching against greed and corruption, he was sent into permanent exile in a foreign country. He was never allowed to return. As he was about to board the ship that was to carry him away for the last time, he finished his farewell speech to the people with the words, "Glory be to God for everything! Glory be to God for everything!"

Perhaps a reference to the exchange of marriage promises might bring all this down to everyday reality. When people exchange these vows, they commit themselves "for better or worse." Most people, when saying these words, are probably hoping that it will always be "better," rather than "worse." But even in a very good marriage, the "worse" will surely come. The point I am making is that the "worse" will be at least as important as the "better." Both are necessary for growing in love, because, in the better times, people learn the joy of loving and sharing their lives together, and, in the worse times, they learn to love unselfishly. The 'worse' may eventually be seen as being as precious as the 'better,' because it can lead us to a deeper, stronger kind of loving.[1]

Is that an impossible attitude for us? I hope not, because when we learn to thank God for everything, we will become more aware that God's blessings are sometimes hidden in loss and suffering, we will experience his presence in deeper ways, and we will be blessed with inner peace.

---

[1] This point is made in Thomas H. Green, SJ, op.cit., p. 104.

If faith is to survive in the modern world,
it will have to be based on the experience of God

In today's Gospel, Jesus tells his disciples to pray and never lose heart. But surprisingly, he seems to be close to losing heart himself when he says, "When the Son of Man comes, will he find any faith on earth?" We all ask similar questions when we're having serious doubts about something. It would seem therefore that Jesus' words are meant, not only for his disciples, but also for himself. In reminding them that God will never abandon the cry of his chosen ones, Jesus is also reassuring himself of his Father's faithfulness. Since he was preaching a message that was in some ways radically new, there were probably a number of occasions when people were struggling to accept what Jesus was saying, or even rejected it outright. That was what happened, for example, after he had spoken about the Eucharist. Many of his disciples could not accept his teaching, and walked away. We're told that Jesus on that occasion turned to the Twelve and asked, "Do you want to leave me too?"

As we look around our world today and reflect upon the state of Christian faith, we may also be tempted to lose heart. The world is changing rapidly. There was a time when we used to speak of Christian countries, but today, it is hardly possible to speak of any countries as Christian any more. Every country is missionary. We live in a post-Christian society. Nations where the Christian faith is integrated with the local culture seem to be things of the past. Many people either have discarded belief altogether, or, they pay only lip-service to it, while living as if there were no God. A journalist, commenting not long ago on the growing expectation that scientists will soon be able to clone a human being, added the remark that "then we will finally be able to do away with the idea of God." For many people around the world, the human race is coming of age today. We are now in charge of our own destiny. We can create our own future, so praying to God is a waste of time. In light of that, we may all sometimes feel like asking ourselves, as Jesus did, "When the Son of Man comes, will he find faith on earth?"

The challenge and test of this situation is first of all, as Jesus said, not to lose heart. But it goes further than that — it is a challenge to deepen our faith. A superficial faith may not be sufficient to carry us through. Theologian Karl Rahner once wrote that, if faith is to survive in the modern world, it will have to come from the experience of God. That's something for us to think about. How many of us can say that we have experienced God? For many people, the Church is just an organization they have joined for the sake of getting to heaven, if they obey its rules. Experiencing God is not something they have ever thought about, or wished for. And yet, the kind of faith that simply obeys the rules in order to get to heaven has no life in it.

If we look around us with the eyes of faith, we will come to recognize that the Spirit of God is indeed present and active in our world. For example, one could see God's plan in the sudden end of the Soviet Union, and the sudden end of apartheid in South Africa. One can also observe the work of the Spirit in the movements towards reconciliation and unity in recent history. It's not so long ago since the countries of Europe were torn apart by war. Now they are coming together in a close political union that has been growing larger in recent times. We can also see the work of the Spirit in the growing awareness among people and governments of the demands of justice around the world, and in the acknowledgment by an increasing number of wealthy nations that they should help the poorer ones by remitting their crushing debts.

What about the presence of the Spirit in our own lives? We need to develop a sharper awareness for the traces of God's presence in every area of human activity and experience. The language of God is the experience that God writes into our lives. The deepest yearnings of our hearts   our yearnings for love, our hopes for peace, our longings for community — these are messages from the God who made us this way. When we come to know ourselves more deeply, and become more deeply aware of our relationship with God, we will become free to sense the movement of God in our lives. And, when we stay close to God, we will come to know our own truth — that is, we will be able to distinguish between what is good for us and what would destroy us. We will recognize the touch of the Spirit in the things that produce peace and joy within us.

So, the struggle for faith has not been lost in today's world — it has simply moved to different areas. It's not enough any more to count the number of hosts consumed at Mass to measure the effectiveness of the Church's preaching and teaching. It will be necessary also to find people who are experiencing the touch of God in their lives, and are willing to be guided by it, and people who are committed to struggle for such things as unity, reconciliation and justice between peoples and nations. Can we be counted among those people? Only we ourselves can answer that question.

Si 35:12-14, 16-18   2 Tm 4:6-8, 16-18   Lk 18:9-14

The tax collector was a genuine human being; the Pharisee was not

The Pharisee and the tax collector are not just people who lived long ago. They are models of people's behavior — perhaps our own, or that of someone we know — that are valid for all times. They represent two very different types — the Pharisee is that kind of person who has carefully observed the law and done the correct thing all his life. Things have gone well with him — he has prospered. And, as often happens with these kind of people, he has made a connection between his correct, law-abiding life and his prosperity. God has rewarded him, he has concluded, for his proper behavior. God has blessed him because he has faithfully observed all the regulations of the Law — because, in short, he is a better person than many others who have little respect for the Law, such as the tax collector standing nearby. He is not even aware of his own self righteousness and arrogance. The tax collector's prayer on the other hand is very different. He knows well where he stands before God, and his prayer reflects that knowledge: "O God, be merciful to me, a sinner."

As we listen to this story, we must wonder sometimes at the kind of people who get a good press in the Gospels, and are singled out for positive comment in its pages: people such as tax collectors, prostitutes, Samaritans — who were looked upon as half-Jews and law breakers; a Roman centurion, who represented the foreign power that was occupying the country; blind people; a leper who came back to thank Jesus for his healing; and other marginal types. Why is it that these people were singled out for positive comment by Jesus, while those who were careful to observe the Law were often criticized? Two things come to mind:

The people who were looked upon as sinners and outsiders had some basic self-knowledge. They had no illusions about themselves, or where they stood in relation to the Law. The centurion, for example, knew that he wasn't worthy even to have Jesus enter his house. The prostitutes and sinners knew that they needed to repent. These people were genuine human beings. They were honest with themselves, and honest with Jesus. They didn't wear masks of respectability. They knew that if God were to accept them, it would be because of his mercy, and not on account of anything they themselves had done. In spite of their sins, they still felt a need for God, they knew what spiritual emptiness was all about, and they were still open to the world of the spirit. Therefore there was still room for God to enter their lives. In other words, they were ready to grow spiritually.

The Pharisee, on the other hand, represented a group of people who were satisfied with themselves. They were not conscious of sin. In their own eyes, they were the righteous people, and their goodness was self-evident because God had rewarded them for it. They thanked God for making them such good people, different from the others. Their righteousness consisted in strict observance of the Law. They saw no need to change anything — they thought they were doing fine just as they were. There was no openness to change — why should they change, when everything was going well for them, as they saw it? They were closed to any possibility that God might see things differently. They could not accept that Jesus might have come from God, or that he had anything to offer them. Jesus had some very sharp things to say about Pharisees and lawyers. He compared them to the tombs of the dead — beautiful on the outside, but inside, full of rottenness and dead people's bones.

Is there something we can take away from this story? If we were to compare ourselves with the Pharisee on the one hand, and the tax collector on the other, most of us would probably fall somewhere in the middle. We are not quite as arrogant as the Pharisee, but neither are we as honest and humble about ourselves as the tax collector. We would benefit from having something less of the Pharisee, and something more of the tax collector. In other words, we need to take an honest look at ourselves and our sins, acknowledge how little we have done with what God has given us, and pray often the prayer of the tax-collector, "O God, be merciful to me, a sinner."

Rv 7:2-4, 9-14   1 Jn 3:1-3   Mt 5:1-12a

These people have learnt the mystery of the Cross

At the heart of every Christian community's life are faithful people
— people who work, people who pray, people who suffer, people
who serve. These are the leaven in the dough, the salt of the earth,
the light on the mountain-top. They appear to be ordinary people
like ourselves — they look and dress in quite an ordinary way, they
drive ordinary looking cars, live in ordinary homes — in fact, they
don't have anything extraordinary about them from society's point
of view. But they *are* extraordinary people. It's not easy to describe
what that extraordinary quality is. Perhaps it's partly in the absence
of some things. They don't seem to need what many others need —
success, or public recognition or gratitude, for example. They're un-
obtrusive people. But others know certain things about them — for
instance, that, if they have a problem, they will be there for them —
that they can rely completely on them in times of need. Even if it
demands a sacrifice, they will still be there to help them. People know
too that their homes are good places to visit, because there's peace
there, and that peace is like a blessing that comes to all who enter.
There's a healing quality that these people have; it's present where
they live, and others can feel it.

It's not that they are seen praying in the church more often than
others, or that they are the more generous contributors. Perhaps the
best way to describe it is that, in some way, these people seem to
have learnt the mystery of the Cross. There's been suffering in their
lives, but it hasn't made them bitter. In some way, they were aware
that the Lord was holding their hand, walking beside them, through
their periods of suffering. That didn't take the pain away, but it carried them through the fiery furnace. They were open to what God
wanted to do with them. Because of that, God worked in them in a
certain way, God did something with them, God's invisible grace
changed them and they learnt the compassion of the Kingdom. If
you were to ask them what made them different, they would not
understand the question, because they don't lay claim to any spe-

cial status. They would identify strongly with Mother Teresa's statement, "God didn't call me to be successful. He called me to be faithful." They're very comfortable with that word, 'faithful.'

Because the Cross has been in their lives, they know how to have compassion. Their compassion is like a light shining out from within them — a light that's kept burning by faith and hope, but above all by love. It's a light that burns with strength and courage. As these people grow older, they are like the wick on a candle that's burning down, that gets lengthier as the last piece of wax melts, and puts out a larger, warmer flame as it comes towards the end. It's the same with their compassionate love.

Another characteristic of these people is wisdom. It's not that they seem to know many things. But they seem to have digested their faith and its implications for their lives better than most. They have an intuitive wisdom that comes from their strong faith that guides them and gives them courage when they're in the shadow of evil, so that they remain untouched by it.

These are the saints of our times, and of every time. It's because of such people, and the witness of their lives, that we, who observe them, can be sure that life is not simply one problem after another, or a question without an answer. The fullness of life that they generously share with others is a demonstration of the fact that life is a gift, life is a mystery, during the course of which we are gradually taken hold of and possessed by the mystery of God's generous and eternal love.

Our late Holy Father, Pope John Paul II canonized hundreds of saints, from all walks of life. A number of them lived in recent times. One of the things he tried to teach the Church through these canonizations is that sainthood is not something removed from ordinary life. Many of the saints recently canonized were lay people who lived out their lives in our day-to-day world — who embraced and loved our world with all its tensions and pressures. This feast of All Saints celebrates their lives. It's also a celebration of holiness in the lives of many ordinary, nameless people, and of our own efforts to be faithful too.

From Jesus' point of view, the tax collector was not unclean at all

We all like a story where the underdog gets affirmed, and the one who has been rejected and cast out is once more included. That's probably because there's a part of us that identifies with the underdog, and so, as we reflect on the story of Zacchaeus, we can feel affirmed by the Lord and included too. There are a number of interesting things about this narrative — Zacchaeus' spiritual hunger, for example. He was a rich man, but his wealth hadn't brought him inner security or peace. He was looking for something more than riches, so he came to see Jesus. The story emphasizes how anxious he was to see the Lord. As the chief tax collector, he was surely no longer a young man, but he hauled himself up into the tree anyway, no doubt panting and perspiring as he did so, in order to get a good look at Jesus. He had no desire to push through the crowd and draw attention to himself — tax collectors were not popular figures — but he was determined to see Jesus one way or another.

Jesus came by and looked up at Zacchaeus. He told him to hurry down, because he was going to stay at his house that day. Zacchaeus came down quickly and welcomed him. We can see from this part of the story that Jesus lets him know, not only that he would *like* to stay with him, but that he strongly desires it — he tells him to "hurry down." There is a contrast drawn here between Jesus' warm and friendly feelings towards the tax collector and his strong desire to be a guest in his house, and the critical reaction of the crowd once they hear what is going to happen — they all begin to murmur and complain that he was going to the home of a sinner. We need to bear in mind that the people despised tax collectors, not simply because of their work, but because they were collecting financial support either for the occupying Roman administration, or for the local Jewish ruler, who was not looked upon as legitimate. It is clear from the crowd's opposition that they do not understand Jesus or his mission to reach out to those who were outcasts and marginalized. Tax collecting was an 'unclean' occupation, that is, it made a person unfit to participate in worship, so they expected Jesus to stay away from a tax collector. But for Jesus, what made a person unclean in the sight of God was what came from the heart. It had rather to do with a person's spiritual state. Therefore he had no problem going into Zacchaeus' home — in fact, he was anxious to go there, because, from Jesus' point of view, the tax collector was not unclean at all. He was, in fact, a good man.

The story proceeds by way of invitation and response. As soon as Jesus announces his intentions, Zacchaeus "quickly" descends from the tree, and welcomes him with delight. He had come there in the first place seeking the Lord, and Jesus, recognizing what was in his heart, had responded with friendship and warmth. Zacchaeus now joyfully responds in turn to Jesus' offer to spend some time in his company. The critics and nay-sayers are then refuted by Zacchaeus' statement that he gives one half of his possessions to the poor and repays fourfold anyone who has been overcharged. Now we understand more clearly why Jesus greeted him and invited himself to his house — Zacchaeus is a kindred spirit — he loves the poor. We must take note of the fact that he actually said that he gave "half" of his belongings to them! What kind of a person gives half of his wealth to the poor? How many people are that generous? Here indeed was a very special person. No wonder Jesus recognized him as a true "son of Abraham." Now we can understand too why Zacchaeus had sought Jesus out. Although he had been ostracized by the people, and excluded from worship in the Temple, his loving heart had led him to Jesus, the living temple of God's love. There were no barriers between Jesus and this man — there was only recognition and acceptance and love.

There's a time in all our lives when the Holy Spirit prompts us to climb a tree — in other words, to do something beyond what we ordinarily do, and look for Jesus. But most people probably don't do it. They're too busy, or too concerned about what demands might be made of them if they did. But those of us who take time to reflect on this Gospel cannot but be moved by the story of Zacchaeus, a man who was physically small but large of heart, who climbed a tree to see Jesus, and will be remembered for that until the end of time.

Defining moments in life reveal what kind of a person I really am

It's very unlikely that any of us will be called upon to face the possibility of dying for what we believe, though that still sometimes happens to priests and religious today in certain countries. But there are, however, many people around who would risk their lives in certain circumstances. There was an article in a newspaper not long ago about a policeman who was leaning over the side of a bridge to grab a young man who had just jumped off. Then the policeman was carried over too, but another person grabbed his foot and hauled them both in. Later, the policeman was asked why he was willing to risk death in order to save a stranger. He responded: "If I didn't try to save him, I couldn't have lived with myself — I could never have been happy again." These kind of incidents happen quite frequently. People sometimes drown trying to rescue others from drowning; others die trying to rescue people, even strangers, from burning houses.

The first reading for today's Mass takes us back to the second century before Christ, when the Syrian king, Antiochus IV, who counted Israel among his dominions, ordered all his subjects to renounce their own religion and worship false gods. Soldiers of the king went around from village to village, torturing and killing those who refused to obey the king's orders. Many people avoided the issue by running away and hiding in the mountains. Others obeyed the king. For all the Jews, it was a time of great crisis in their lives. They had to make a choice — they had to search deep within and ask themselves what their religious commitment really meant to them. Was that commitment precious enough to endure death or flight into the mountains for its sake? How much did it really mean to them? For the remainder of their lives they would have to live with that decision. It was a defining moment for each of them.

These defining moments in life are not confined to such situations. Most people, I believe, sooner or later are faced with decisions that determine the direction of their subsequent lives. These may be decisions — seemingly minor decisions — that are repeated over and over, for example. Or it may be a clear decision that is sharply defined — having to do with the kind of lifestyle a person chooses, or the kind of values a person lives by, or a person's response to the requirements of faith. Sometimes it may be that a person does not consciously make a decision. But not to decide is also to decide.

The fact is that life demands of us, sooner or later, that we affirm, at least by how we choose to live, and how we choose to interact with other people, what kind of people we are, and what we really believe in. The direction we choose will be important for whether we live or die spiritually — and spiritual death can arrive a long time before physical death. This is the issue that that policeman was talking about. There are defining moments in everybody's life — in his case a sharply defined one when the choice was very clear — when we can go one way or the other, and these moments define who we really are.

Let me tell you a story. Albert Camus, the French writer and philosopher, once wrote a short story[1] about a man he met in a bar in Amsterdam, who told him the story of his life. The man used to be a very successful lawyer in Paris. He was a well-known figure, and was looked up to by many people as an example and a model for others. But there was another side to him that no one knew about, a side that was played out under cover of darkness, and was marked by unfaithfulness, lies and debauchery. But all that didn't trouble him. This continued for many years until, one night, in the early hours of the morning, he was crossing one of those narrow footbridges that span the river Seine in a number of places. He passed a woman on the bridge. She was leaning over the side, looking down into the water. Suddenly, as he reached the other side, he heard a movement behind him, a sound of splashing water, and a cry for help. He hesitated, looked around for a moment, then walked quickly away. But he found, once he had returned home, that he could not forget those sounds. And, as he continued to reflect on the incident, all of a sudden he found himself confronted by his own reality — the kind of person he really was — the kind of self-centered, uncaring, ruthless person he had become over the years. He was confronted by the evil and hypocrisy in his life, and what it had done to him. And now he was sitting in a bar in Amsterdam, talking to anyone who would listen, hoping that he could ease his terrible burden of guilt. As he had stood on that bridge over the Seine, he had arrived at a defining moment in his life — a moment that symbolized, in a way he couldn't deny any more to himself, the kind of person he had become.

Do we have such defining moments in our lives? Certainly we do. Those moments may not be sharply defined, as with the policeman or the man on the bridge; it may be a series of moments, a series of relatively minor decisions leading in a certain direction. But, when all is said and done, that moment or that series of minor decisions are defining right now what kind of a person we really are — they are moving us towards spiritual life, or spiritual death.

---

[1] *The Fall*, by Albert Camus.

THIRTY-THIRD SUNDAY IN ORDINARY TIME
Ml 3:19-20a   2 Th 3:7-12   Lk 21:5-19

The battle between sin and grace continues, both in our world and within ourselves

Today's Gospel presents us with a grim picture — the destruction of the Jerusalem Temple, wars and insurrections, earthquakes, plagues and famines, false predictions of the end of the world, and persecutions of Jesus' disciples. But there is also a positive side to the story. His disciples will refuse to listen to the false prophets, nor will they be frightened by all these events. The eloquence and wisdom that God will give them will be such that no one will be able to refute their words, and their endurance to the end will be rewarded with God's special care, and eternal life. Although some of the events described in this account, such as the destruction of the Temple, may be ascribed to a certain date and time, the general picture that Jesus presents here is in fact applicable to the whole course of Christian history. In other words, these events — wars, earthquakes, plagues and famines, and the courageous response of Jesus' disciples, have continued to occur throughout history right up to our own day. They symbolize and represent the interaction of sin and grace in human life. Every generation is conscious of that interaction — the presence of terrible evil in the hearts of people, while, at the same time, goodness and love are never completely wiped out.

We can see that consciousness being expressed, for example, in modern art and literature. There is a small, but famous, art gallery in the heart of Madrid (Spain's capital city), that houses only one piece of art. The picture is Pablo Picasso's 'Guernica.' The huge painting goes from wall to wall at one end of the gallery. Many visitors sit down and look at it for a long time. Guernica was a peaceful village in northern Spain that was bombed and destroyed by the Germans in 1937, during the Spanish Civil War, and its inhabitants wiped out. It's a horror picture of men, women, children, animals and disembodied heads, expressing fear, disbelief and horror. The picture seems to mark the end of an era, and the beginning of a new age when human life, even that of children, would be cheaper than ever it was before. It's a picture that seems to shout at the observer, "Who are you and what stand are you taking about all this?" It portrays the dark side of the Modern Era with all its indiscriminate violence — and of the revulsion and alienation it generates, even in animals.

Maybe some of you some of you have heard of the short-story writer, Flannery O'Connor. She was a convert to Catholicism, and had a deep sense of the surprising ways God's grace is present in human affairs. A constant theme in her stories is 'grace and alienation,' in other words, the incredible intervention of God's grace in human situations that are touched by evil. One of her stories is called *A Good Man Is Hard to Find*. It's about an old grandmother, her son, his wife and their children who fall victim to a psychopathic killer, recently escaped from prison, who overtakes them after their car accident on a lonely country road. The killer and his men quietly walk the family members into the woods and shoot them, one by one. The grandmother, who is the last to be shot, attempts till the end to talk the killer down, to try to convince him that he is a good man, and that good people don't do these things. But the killer knows he is not a good man. He has been cut off — alienated — from the rest of the world and doesn't know how to become rejoined. He calls himself "the Misfit." But in spite of that, the old woman seems to be making some progress. A change suddenly comes over the man. His voice begins to break, and the grandmother sees his face, close to her own, as if he were going to cry. She reaches out and touches him compassionately on the shoulder and says, "Why, you're one of my babies — you're one of my own children." But the Misfit springs back as if a snake had bitten him and shoots her three times.

It's a story about a terrible tragedy, but in some awful way it was a moment of triumph for the old woman. The darkness and fear she had experienced during the murder of her family had lifted for a moment, and she suddenly saw the Misfit from the perspective of God's Kingdom. She saw what most people don't see — what she herself had missed all her life — that there are no misfits, no out-casts in that Kingdom. In a moment of burning insight — a moment of grace — she discovered the Kingdom, and entered it.

We live at a time when the bombing of cities has become en-tertainment on the evening news, and videos of people being be-headed may be viewed on the Internet and downloaded. But con-trasting with those horrors of our age are the Christian witness of a Mother Teresa of Calcutta, of the martyred Archbishop Oscar Romero of El Salvador and of countless other people, that testifies to the reality of sacrificial love in our world. The picture of the hu-man situation that Jesus drew long ago hasn't changed in its essen-tials — sin and grace will always be present in human life. Evil will surely touch us, but grace is never far away.

CHRIST THE KING
2 S 5:1-3   Col 1:12-20   Lk 23:35-43

*The Church is going through a death experience, that it might rise
again to become something new*

In a play by Tennessee Williams called *Suddenly Last Summer*, there's
a scene that describes thousands of turtles coming ashore on a de-
serted beach to lay their eggs and bury them above the waterline
for hatching. A few months later, one hundred thousand baby turtles
are making their way down to the water. But all of a sudden, the sky
is darkened by a huge number of flesh-eating birds as they swoop
down, turn the turtles over and eat them alive. Very few turtles make
it to the water.

The first half of life can be like that for many people — a race
to the water — in other words, a race to succeed, to gain the possessions and status that are considered important in life. But on the
way, they get eaten alive by life's experiences — the painful ones
that can make them bitter — the losses that leave them feeling empty
— the mistakes that leave them feeling foolish — the pleasures that
seem so desirable but pass so quickly — the love that doesn't last.
Some people arrive at the final stage of their lives still wondering
what it was really all about. On this feast of Christ the King, we have
arrived at the final stage of the Church's year. It's a time to reflect
together on what that might mean for us. And what the Church puts
before us to assist our reflection is a world away from the race to
succeed. It seems like the very opposite, in fact — it's the image of
Jesus hanging on a Cross beneath the inscription, "This is the King
of the Jews." We are presented with a king, not in splendor, but a
king in darkness, a king in disgrace, hanging between two criminals.

Darkness and disgrace have touched the Church's life over the
past twenty years in ways that it has never previously experienced.
Perhaps because of that, and for other reasons too, the gap between
Church and world appears to be widening, and the Church's moral
authority seems to be decreasing. This situation gives us an opportunity to identify more closely with the Cross of our disgraced king,

with his weakness and apparent failure. It seems to me that the Church in these times is being called by the Lord to a death-experience, that it may rise again, as it has in the past, to become something new. Anyone who is growing in faith will experience times of spiritual darkness, when the Lord seems to be far away. These times of darkness are sent by him to break us away from our own self-will and to detach us from what we cling to, so that we might be ready to do what *he* wants, rather than what *we* want. In darkness we experience helplessness, and we come to realize how much we depend on God. Spiritual darkness is a time of purification.

This time of darkness in the life of the universal Church community is perhaps such a time too — a time of purification and letting-go — a time for Church leaders to embrace a simpler, humbler way of life and a gentler way of exercising authority, and a time to give stronger witness to the Lord's compassion and love. The exercise of power and control in the Church needs to be constantly evaluated in the light of the Gospel. Perhaps you have heard the saying, "When love retreats, power advances." The Christ who reigned from the Cross was bereft of all earthly power. There were no pomp and circumstance as the God of love emptied himself on Calvary. On the Cross, his witness of perfect love stood out alone. The only exercise of kingship from the Cross was an exercise of compassion — "This day you will be with me in paradise." All that remained there was the power of the Spirit that Jesus handed down to the Church at his death. We need more of the Spirit's power in the Church today, and of the kind of kingship that Jesus exercised from the Cross.

The image of Jesus as king that today's Gospel puts before us is stark and desolate, warmed only by the compassion of his words to the repentant thief. It's not at all attractive, but it confronts us with the reality of the Gospel — a reality that may not fit very well with the values we ourselves have chosen to live by. The Cross of Christ is a powerful sign today for the whole, universal Catholic community. It reminds us that Jesus reigned from the Cross, and that new life for the Church will not come apart from our embracing of the Cross, as individuals and as a community.